GATHERING WHAT THE GREAT NATURE PROVIDED

'Ksan. *Photo: Hilary Stewart*

Gathering What the Great Nature Provided

Food Traditions of the Gitksan

By the People of 'Ksan
Drawings by Hilary Stewart

Douglas & McIntyre
Vancouver
University of Washington Press
Seattle

This book is dedicated to Steven Morrison of Kispiox, B.C., 1902 – 1978, who gave us, among other valuable memories, the beautiful phrase, Gathering What the Great Nature Provided.

Copyright © 1980 by Kitanmax–'Ksan Publications

All rights reserved. No part of this book may be reproduced or transmitted in any form by any means without permission in writing from the publisher, except by a reviewer, who may quote brief passages in a review.

Published in Canada by Douglas & McIntyre Ltd., 1615 Venables Street, Vancouver, British Columbia.

Canadian Cataloguing in Publication Data:

Main entry under title:
Gathering what the great nature provided

ISBN 0-88894-249-4

1. Kitksan Indians—Food.   2. Indians of North America—Food.
E99.K55G38   641.3'008997   C80-091183-0

Published simultaneously in the United States of America by the University of Washington Press, Seattle, under arrangement with Douglas & McIntyre Ltd.

Library of Congress Cataloging in Publication Data:

People of 'Ksan.
  Gathering what the great nature provided

  1. Kitksan Indians—Food.   2. Indians of North America—British Columbia—Food.   3. Cookery, Indian.   I. Title.
E99.K55P46   1980   394.1'2'08997   79-3871
ISBN 0-295-95710-7

Designed by Robert Bringhurst Ltd., Vancouver. Composition by The Typeworks, Mayne Island, British Columbia. Printed & bound in the United States of America by Kingsport Press.

The publisher acknowledges the support of the British Columbia Heritage Trust in the preparation of this book.

Contents

Introduction   9

1. GATHERING WHAT THE GREAT NATURE PROVIDED   11

Cooking Methods in General   15

Boiling   15 / Earth-oven Baking   17 / Baking in Ashes   18 / Roasting & Barbecuing   18 / Toasting   19

Preservation & Storage of Food   20

Smoking & Drying   20 / Earthen Cellars   22 / Storage Houses   25 / Wooden Food Caches   25 / Dry Storage   27 / Aging   27 / Oolichan Grease as a Preservative   27 / Birch Bark   27

2. THE FOOD WE ATE   29

Fish   30

Barbecuing   32 / Yoos Hun   32 / Cooking Fish Heads   33 / Drying Fish   34 / Smoking Fish   36 / Fish Strips   41 / Ts'okxw   41 / Fish Eggs   42 / Fish Eyes   43 / Geekx   43 / Smoked Heads   43 / Backbones   44 / T'ul   44 / Oolichan   44 / Other Foods from the Sea   44

Meat & Fowl   45

Cooking & Smoking   46 / Cooking Grease   49 / Salmon Grease   50

Berries & Fruit   51

Soapberries   48 / Huckleberries   66 / Saskatoons   66 / Cranberries & Crab Apples   66 / Salmonberries   68 / Stonecrop   68 / Frogberries   68 / Blueberries   68 / High Bush Blueberries   68 / Elderberries   70 / Indian Glads   70 / Bunchberries   70 / Bearberries   70 / Raspberries & Strawberries   72 / Thornberries   72 / Pincherries & Chokecherries   72 / Rose Hips   74 / Gooseberries & Black Currants   74 / Thimbleberries   74 / 'Witsxw Maa'y   74 / Dayks   74 / Hlayax   76 / Nisk'o'o   76

Tubers, Bulbs, Roots, Bark & Greens 77

Wild Rice 77 / *A<u>x</u>* 77 / *Pine Noodles* 80 / *Hemlock Sapwood* 83 / *Fireweed* 86 / *Wild Rhubarb* 86 / *Wild Onions* 86 / *Greens* 87 / *Nuts* 87 / *Gum* 87 / *Water Lily Roots* 87

Oolichan Grease from the Nass 89

Making Oolichan Grease 91 / *Drying Oolichans* 92

Beverages, Soups & Syrups 94

Soups 94 / *Horsetail Reed Juice* 94 / *Various Teas* 95 / *Fireweed & Other Syrups* 95

Other Edible Plants 96

Foods of Our Ancestors 96

Food After the Europeans Came 96

Bread & Bannock 99 / *Potatoes* 99 / *New Foods, New Words* 100

3. SOME HINTS FOR COOKS 101

Soups 102

Fishbone Soup 102 / *Fish Chowder* 102 / *Village Soup* 103

Breads 103

Pan Bread 103 / *Bannock & Bannock-Style Bread* 103 / *Fried Bread* 104

Fish 104

Baked Fish Heads 104 / *Buts'* 105 / *Fish Hearts* 105 / *Boiled Fish Backbone* 105 / *Salted Fish* 105 / *Toasted Half-dried Fish* 105 / *Boiled Fully Dried Salmon* 106 / *Salted Fish Belly* 106 / *Fried Seaweed* 106

Fish Eggs 106

Herring Eggs 106 / *Boiled Fish Eggs & Seaweed* 106 / *Fried Herring Eggs* 107 / *Fish Eggs & Oolichan Grease* 107 / *Toasted Seaweed* 107

Meat   107

> *Boiled Moose Nose*   107 / *Smoked & Roasted Porcupine*   108
> *Roast Rabbit Ears*   108 / *Fried Rabbit Innards*   108 /
> *Barbecued Beaver Tail*   108 / *Half-Smoked Bear Intestines*   109
> *Boiled Moose Intestines*   109 / *Roast Marrow*   109
> *Mountain Goat Tripe*   109 / *Wild Meat*   109

Desserts   110

> *Yal Is*   110 / *Sun-dried Soapberries*   110 / *Dayks*   110

4. FOOD IN OUR LIVES   111

Etiquette   112

How Food Shaped the Way of the Gitksan   114

> *Food as Intermediary with the Powers Beyond*   115 / *Food for the Dead*   117 / *Food as a Symbol*   117 / *Food & Fun*   119

APPENDICES   121

The Writing System   122

Terminology   124

Acknowledgements   127

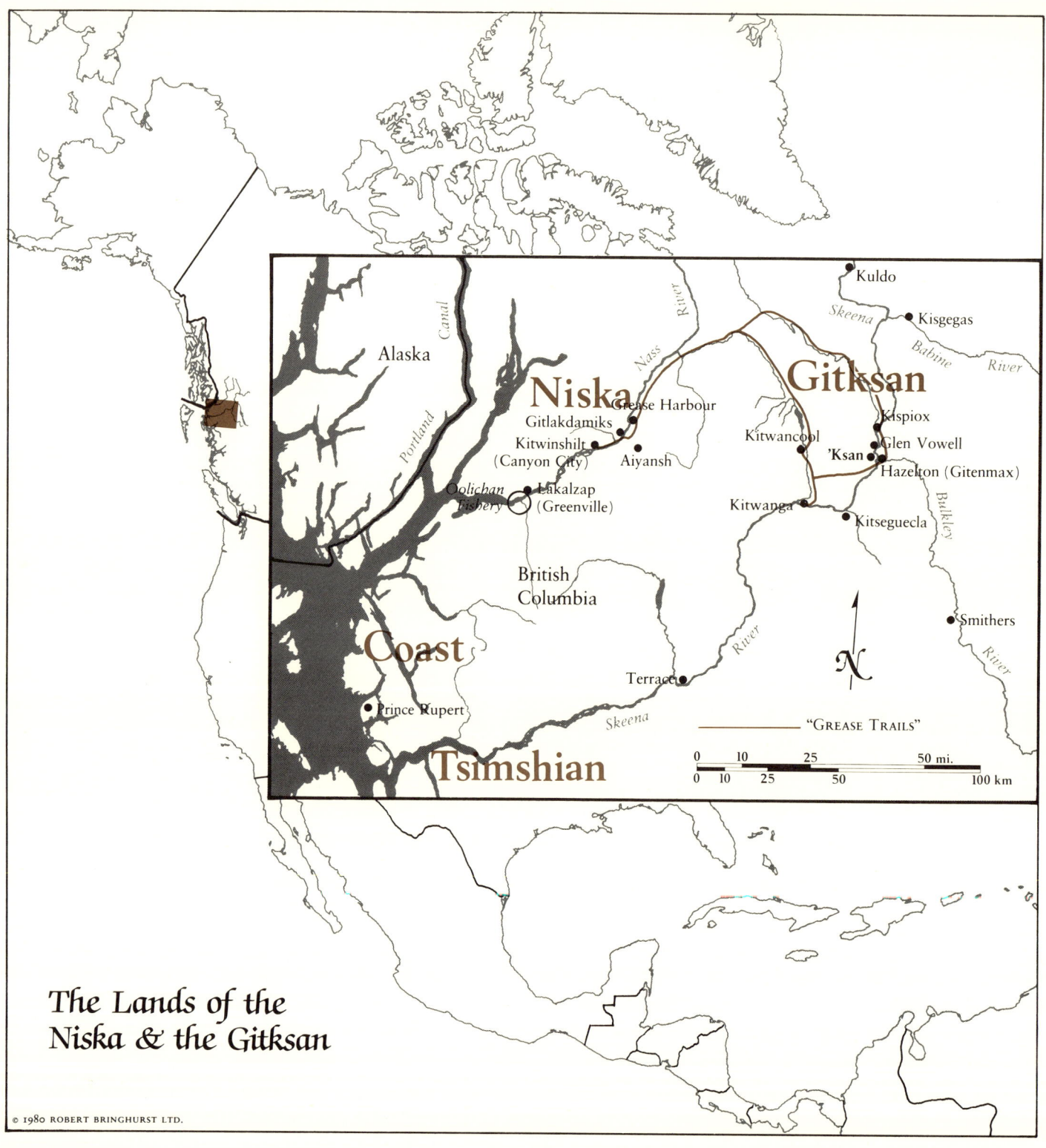

The Lands of the Niska & the Gitksan

Introduction

'KSAN is an Indian museum and craft village on the banks of the Skeena River (the 'Ksan) in north-central British Columbia. Our race is called Gitksan—the people of the 'Ksan River.

Because the territories of our chiefs were not on the main routes of the traders and settlers, the European civilization did not engulf us at an early date. So our elders still hold considerable knowledge of the histories, habits and techniques of their great-great-grandfathers. We use the village of 'Ksan as a window through which those of us today, especially our children, may glimpse most aspects of the culture that our ancestors enjoyed.

In 1971 some of 'Ksan's people, aided by a government grant, began to record the wealth of information still stored in the memories of the elders. The results encouraged them to persist in the quest, with the result that today an invaluable historical file has been amassed.

We have it in our hearts to create from this treasure a series of books so that our young people can know the stature of their heritage—and share it with the world. This book is the second in the series; the first was a book of legends about the trickster-transformer We-gyet (Weget).

All of our writing is done by consensus. More than ninety people—known as the Book Builders—helped with this book. First, we tape-recorded, in our language, information from knowledgeable Gitksan elders about our food traditions. This information was translated into English, then classified and organized under the headings we hoped to cover. Next, a group of from three to eight discussed the material and weighed its pertinence and accuracy. If gaps were discovered, or if contradictory information had been given, we sought more data. Finally, the new information was evaluated by a consensus group and the acceptable versions incorporated into a new, fairly cohesive whole. At least two informed people read this version, making corrections where necessary. We describe this process to indicate that the book was indeed built step-by-step, and we hope that its publication will draw out corrections and further information.

We do not single out individuals in the body of the book, for we always work as a group. The names of all who helped—authors, informants, researchers, typists—are listed alphabetically on the last page.

As you read, you will discover that we move from past tense to present tense at will. We have used the present tense when talking about something which we still do and the past tense if the custom has been dropped.

Because our language is fast slipping into an "old way," we have included a list of Gitksan terms used in *Gathering What the Great Nature Provided,* as well as a brief summary of the writing system used to transcribe these words into our own language. This system is presently in a state of flux, but we hope that students of language will be able to cope with its inconsistencies and that all Gitksan will "get the drift."

THE BOOK BUILDERS OF 'KSAN
April 1980

1

Gathering What the Great Nature Provided

"IN THE OLDEN DAYS all our people had to do to get food was to gather what the Great Nature provided," said one of the wisest of the elders who supplied the facts for this book. "There was no need for our ancestors to work at gardens, because so many roots and berries and plants just grow here. There was no need to grow beef or pigs, because lots of goats, caribou, deer, groundhog, porcupine and beaver lived close by, on the mountains, in the woods or along the edges of the rivers and lakes. There was no need, like now, to go down to the coast for fish, because we'd lots of our own good fish right here. Besides, ducks, geese, grouse and even swans flew where we could trap them.... There were tons of berries, just tons, every year."

"It was a good time," agreed another elder. "It was a good time."

"But we have a long, cold winter when ice fishing is uncertain, most birds have flown south and nothing that's edible grows except meat, and you can't stay healthy on meat. We needed a pile of food to get us through the winter, so we spent our summers working like slaves to get it stored away. There was lots going on in the winter, too, that we needed extra food for—feasts that lasted a month, maybe more, and no one was allowed to be out hunting or trapping when a big feast was on, or when *Nax Nok* hit [when the Cosmic Powers visit]. The work *had* to be done in the summer."

So the gathering and storing of food monopolized the warmer months. The gathering included berry picking, bark and root gathering, hunting, fishing and the trapping of birds and animals. Hunting, fishing and trapping continued throughout the winter but were not pursued every day, because there were winter activities of more importance than food gathering.

"We didn't allow getting food to keep anyone away from a big feast [the so-called potlatch]; those feasts were *the* biggest thing... [we] had to have lots of food to serve and even more to give away for *so'o*—the extra food you get to take home."

Gathering food was hard work, but every minute of it was enjoyable to our people. All our elders smile when they recount their memories of expeditions to the berry patches, hemlock stands and root crop areas. The comradeship and satisfying experience of working unselfishly together outweighed every hardship. Young and old, man and woman, boy and girl, chief and slave—everyone who could walk or who was small enough to be carried in a back cradle joined the food gathering excursions.

Everyone worked. Absolutely everyone. No one wanted to be labelled lazy—that was almost as bad as being called a thief. Besides, starvation

Hole-in-the-Ice Pole at Kitwancool. The bottom figure tells the story of an ancestor who procured an abundance of fish when all in his village were close to starvation.
Photo: Barry Downs

was always a threat. Almost every family has an *adaawk,* or family history, which tells of an ancestor who saved his family or village from starvation by finding food just in the nick of time. If the winter was longer and colder than usual, or if the salmon run was late, or the winter supply of stored food was destroyed by fire, or raiders came from the Nass, or some other calamity occurred, then things could be tough—very tough. This fear of famine spurred all but the useless ones.

The various chores were divided equally according to a person's capacity and ability. There were tiny picking boxes for small children and ten-gallon boxes for the strong men and women. No one walked empty-handed. On a berry gathering expedition, men usually built temporary evergreen shelters, felled trees for drying-rack supports or for new, semi-permanent berry-drying houses (*wilp sa maa'y*), fashioned wooden pounding hammers and hunted or fished while the women and children gathered, cleaned, cooked, dried and stored. However, if the need arose either men or women performed any of the necessary chores.

The happy, busy group stayed out until the work was completed, perhaps three or four weeks, depending on how plentiful the "crop" was or how good the weather for the drying process. Rain was bad news, as it soured the berries on the racks before they could dry. A long rainy period could slow the drying process and keep the gatherers out on the mountain for a long, long time.

Everyone, including the children and pack dogs, helped to carry the food home.

If someone had a misfortune, perhaps spilling a box of berries, then everyone set to work to fill the spilled box again. Slower gatherers were given a hand by the faster ones. (The better hunters likewise shared their take.) Successful food gatherers always divided their supplies with those who for some good reason had had to stay home. When berry pickers returned, a little feast, called *xwitsansxw*—to-give-out-the-crushed-berries—was prepared at which those who had been unable to go picking were guests. Great helpings of berries were served, and each guest was given a sizable portion to take home.

Each picker, child and adult alike, stored her provisions in a spot set aside for her. When winter came and visitors were to be fed, children as well as their mothers brought out their preserved edibles and offered the food to the guests. One informant says, "I had my own little picking basket and my own small storage boxes. Mother helped me dry and roll the berries, but they were mine to give out and I used to feel real proud when I offered guests my own berry cakes or fish that I'd caught. The grownups always praised me a lot."

Boiling food by means of hot stones and wooden boxes

Cooking Methods in General

THE GATHERED FOODS were not only wholesome but also interesting because varied methods of cooking and preparation avoided a monotony of menu. These methods included boiling, toasting, barbecuing, aging, smoking, sun drying, air drying and oven baking.

Boiling

In ancient days, boiling was done by filling bent red cedar boxes with water, then adding heated stones until the water boiled. A second box of water stood close by the stones. Each stone was lifted from the fire with

15

Iron pots at 'Ksan

long wooden tongs and rinsed in the water of the second box before it was placed in the cooking box. These stones were kept neatly piled, ready to be used again and again. The box used for boiling was usually reinforced by encircling it with strong cedar ropes, which gave extra support for its wooden walls.

By 1800 the white traders' iron and brass pots were taking the place of the wooden cooking boxes. The basic name we gave to pots and kettles was one we had used for the old boxes: *anjam,* "a place-where-to-cook-in-water." One dependable informant believes that the iron pot first came to us from early Russian explorers because our name for it literally translates as "place-where-to-cook-in-water-Russian." All sizes and shapes of iron and brass containers have been plentiful in our villages; we have seen iron pots that would hold eight gallons and more.

Earth-oven Baking

Most baking was done in earth ovens. We have been told about three methods of oven construction. In all three a hole is dug and lined with hot stones, about the size and shape of large baking potatoes, but the stone-heating technique varies from baker to baker.

Baker One lines the pit with rocks, builds a big fire in and above the pit, lets the fire die down to embers, "and cleans up any big stuff that might be in the way of the food." Baker Two heats his stones in a big fire outside the pit, then, using tongs, lines the pit with the heated stones. Baker Three builds a good fire in and on top of the pit, then carefully arranges rocks on top of the fire in such a way that, as the fire burns down, the heated rocks slip into place in the pit, finally resting at the bottom on a bed of hot embers. With a stick the cook juggles the fallen rocks into suitable positions to form a hot, even bottom for the earth oven.

The size of the baking pit or oven depends on the size of the roast. "As a rule pits were used to cook big animals or big bunches of stuff like hemlock bark." (See page 83.)

When the hot rocks are in place all bakers sprinkle a thin layer of soil on them for insulation, then cover the soil with a layer of green growth; moss, ferns, skunk cabbage leaves and hemlock boughs have all been mentioned as suitable coverings at this stage.

On this green bed they put the food that is to be baked. "It's likely to be neatly wrapped in birch bark." (Occasionally hemlock bark is used.)

"The birch bark wrapper keeps the food clean and seals it so that the baking food is self basted and the good juices that seep out are saved."

Next, all bakers cover the baking food with another layer of skunk cabbage leaves or other suitable greens, then sprinkle on more soil. The depth of the soil layer depends upon the size and quantity of the food that is being cooked. A big fire is needed to bake a whole mountain goat, so in this case the cook puts on a fairly thick layer of earth insulation between fire and "roast." If a single Dolly Varden is to be baked, only a thin layer of soil will be needed.

The cooks learned by experience how much fire was necessary and how long it should burn in order to bake each kind of food. We are told by one informant that the tasty root *ax* was timed by leaving two inches of the plant's short, curly stem above ground; when the fire had completely demolished the stem, the *ax* was cooked. Similar tests were doubtless known to our grandmothers, but this is the only one in our records. Another informant says that testing was done by scooping the earth away at one corner and taking a peek at the meat, fish or roots. Most people consider this the more reliable test.

Baking pits were used again and again. Suitable stones were piled beside them, or in them, ready for use when more baking was to be done.

Baking in Ashes

"Sometimes they didn't want to wait while food cooked in an earth oven, but they baked right in the ashes. They just scooped out some coals from the campfire or the central fire in the house and put the food in where the coals had been, put some coals back on top and left the food until it cooked. Maybe they wrapped the food in skunk cabbage leaves first. Potatoes are real nice cooked this way—*'mii ooyak'.*"

Roasting & Barbecuing

Roasting or barbecuing is a favourite way of cooking small animals such as porcupine and groundhog, and birds such as grouse, ducks and geese. Roasting can be done on a turning spit made by suspending the dressed carcass from a wet, green willow rope attached to a stake driven firmly into the ground. A cord of green willow leads back to the base of the stake over a fork in the upper end, and the suspended food rotates slowly over the fire. If it becomes motionless, a pull on the cord sets the meat spinning, thus allowing it to roast evenly. Some informants believe this method arrived with the white man.

Roasting or barbecuing is also done by suspending the food over the fire on a green, three- or four-pronged stake whose single, sharpened end has been driven into the ground at a sharp angle. The prongs may skewer the food or they may act as a kind of cradle, in either case holding the food over the fire while the cooking is done. "A wide-forked stake which sort of cradles the food is best because it is easy to turn the food and you don't have to take the stake out of the meat to get the food cooked even."

Yet another method is to run a sharpened stake through the "roast," then rest the ends of the stake on two wooden braces well beyond the heat of the fire.

"The rocks beside a creek or river can be turned into a nice grill. Find a couple of long, flat rocks, or several rocks about the same height, and build your fire between them. Put a stake through the fish and rest the ends of the stake on the rocks. If you put some small sticks [skewers]

across the fish every few inches the fish is easier to turn and stays together better when you flip it over to cook the other side. The little sticks aren't needed if the fish is small, of course."

Toasting

Toasting can be done with a long-handled toasting rack. We show two types. For the first, a single willow withe about one inch in diameter is used. The branches are left on. The top, or small end, is bent back and tied to the main stem, forming a hoop large enough to hold the piece of food to be toasted. Enough small branches to provide adequate support for the food are taken across to the opposite side and tied. Unnecessary branches are then cut off.

A second, more substantial kind of rack requires a forked willow withe with branches. The forked ends are bent back and tied to the stem or handle to form a heart-shaped framework. The branches are then tied to the stem within the framework to give additional support.

These hand-held racks, both of which are called *ha'nii bahla'am ts'al*, can be made on the spot in a few minutes.

A third toaster needs no illustration as it is simply a sturdy branch sharpened to a point at the thinner end. The cook spears the meat with the sharpened stake and holds it over the fire until the food is cooked — a very good method for dried fish or meat.

Willow toasting racks

The old smokehouses at Kisgegas.
Photo: National Museum, Ottawa

Preservation & Storage of Food

BECAUSE IN EARLY DAYS we had to preserve massive quantities of food, our people devised numerous storage and preservation techniques. Some of these are still used. The most common method of preservation is drying—drying until no moisture is left to cause mildew, souring, rot or decay of any sort.

Smoking & Drying

Sun drying and air drying are used, the advantage of these processes being that the food does not have the smoked taste which some people do not enjoy. "Berries sun dry quite easily, but fish are tricky. Sun burns fish, and consequently you either have to turn your drying fish constantly or keep it in the shade.... You also have to see that the drying food does not get wet and that insects and flies are kept away." Several local experts claim that fish cannot be sun dried successfully.

A smokehouse built from cedar posts and split cedar planks, held together with cedar bark rope and roofed with cedar bark shingles

But most of us like the flavour of smoke, and our favourite dryer is the trusty smokehouse. Since the smokehouse was so very reliable and important to our ancestors we will describe it in detail.

A permanent Indian smokehouse is neat, orderly and strongly built. The shadier the location the better, for fish rot in hot places. The sketch shows the main exterior features of an old-style smokehouse. Naturally, smokehouses are situated close to a good fishing spot, which may be far from home or winter village. Small, less elaborate, semipermanent smokehouses are built in the berry patches or hunting grounds.

Within a big smokehouse, separate areas of floor and wall space are allotted to each woman; these are called *ts'im xts'axs*. In past times the smokehouse workers were the wives of the chiefs who owned the territory or fishing holes. Today smokehouses are shared on a more informal basis; they may belong to a single family or to several families.

Each woman arranges for her own wood supply and has her own preference. Punky, slow-burning cottonwood or poplar make a satisfactory fire, giving off lots of smoke and providing a low, steady heat. Rotted poplar is the wood most commonly used. Cottonwood smoke tastes stronger and may hide the flavour of the food that is being dried. Alder, if well rotted, makes a good smokehouse fire and is preferred by many cooks for berry drying. Our neighbours on the coast prefer alder. Because the smoke must not stain nor discolour the food, we never use woods containing a lot of pitch. And we never use red cedar because it makes too hot a fire.

Inside a smokehouse many tiny, neat fires may smoulder or, if only a little meat or fish is being dried, there may be one small central source of smoke. The fire must merely smoulder; it must not be allowed to get hot, except for short controlled periods, or the meat or fish will be ruined. Basically, the fire is a source of smoke, not heat. It also keeps flies away from the food during the slow drying process. "That fire, it's to scare them fly away while the fish dry so slow."

Food can also be dry smoked or half smoked. Dry smoking removes all moisture content from the finished food, leaving the fish or meat as dry and hard as a board. Half-smoked fish or meat is moist and soft, but will not keep very long. Some of the old people wrapped dry-smoked fish in birch bark, then put the package in the walls of their earthen cellars, towards the bottom. The resulting product was juicy and soft; it needed no boiling or added fat to reconstitute it, as did other dry-smoked fish. The wrapping was so carefully done that the smoked fish was almost completely sealed from the air. Some cooks claim to have used this method with half-smoked fish and baked fish as well.

The time required to dry smoke fish depends on the size of the fish and the moisture present in the air. Today, modern deepfreeze and canning methods make half smoking popular.

Earthen Cellars

In ancient times, the Great Nature provided another excellent food storage place, the earthen pit or food storage hole known as *anyuusim yip*. These pits are found in various shapes and sizes. We judge from our records that the white man's shovel with its leverage and efficiency radically changed the basic design of the pit because excavations of storage holes that have not been used for many, many years show a cone-shaped or thimble-shaped hole about three feet in diameter and three to four feet deep. On the other hand, many living elders have described excavations which resemble a white man's root cellar, complete with ladder for access and a rooflike cover. Several instances of "cellars" dug into sidehills are recorded, two of which are still in existence, but we have not been able to determine the antiquity of this type of storage place. The cone-shaped and thimble-shaped holes were usually lined with birch bark; the European-type cellars were sometimes planked on sides and bottom, as were the sidehill cellars. Many people "dug pits for spuds right where the spuds grow."

All the old-style storage holes were situated close to a village, just off a trail. At Old Kuldo, a village that has not been lived in for fifty years,

Sidehill cellar, with packages of food wrapped in birchbark

you can see neat rows of circular depressions which, to the naked eye, seem identical in size and shape, as if they were mechanically made. These are today's markers of the ancient storage pits, neatly arranged alongside the village. We are not sure what tool was used for these excavations. Some say that a sharpened pole was driven into the ground at the centre of the hole-to-be, then rotated in ever widening and deepening circles until a cone-shaped hole resulted.

All the old-type holes were carefully disguised to prevent discovery by two-legged or four-legged thieves. Perhaps there was special emphasis on the four-legged variety, for thievery was not common among our ancestors. The food was wrapped in birch bark and the bundles were placed in the hole, which might be lined with birch bark or with boughs

Entrance to an old storage cellar

of various types. Food parcels were packed to within eight or ten inches of the top, then various coverings were piled on. One of the best was very dry coniferous needles.

"Pile 'em on top, maybe six inches deep. Mice don't like them needle ... no animal like to stick his nose into them needle. Them needle has to be real brown, never green. Us kids used to get sacks of 'em for the *anyuusim yip*."

"In summer, when there's a real dry spell, you go out under the trees and take shovels of those dry needles—they're thick under some trees, inches deep. They're springy to walk on. They are just right to put on top of spuds if you dig them and leave them in the field in holes."

Every precaution was taken to disguise the scent of the food. Earth was piled on top of the needles, boughs or bark. One authority claims that burnt bark was used: "No animal like to go near that burning smell."

The holes were usually opened when the frost was still in the ground, and then completely emptied of their contents, since clean, dry coverings were hard to come by under winter conditions. Besides, there was no food to store, otherwise the storage hole, which was usually there for emergencies, would not have been opened in the first place.

Where a gravel cutbank was available, our canny ancestors converted it into rows of neat storage shelves by forcing birch bark-covered packages into the exposed face of the bank. Informants who are now in their sixties remember "pantries" of birch-covered packages close to the site of 'Ksan.

Sidehill cellars (*anyust*) have been in use as long as any living person can remember. They have been described as "a kind of cave dug out of the hill from the front. You get in from a door-like."

Another informant has said: "I can remember my mother-in-law's cellar. You had to duck your head to go in the door hole. The floor was dirt with planks in some places and there were some planks on the sides. If you stood up straight you got cobwebs in your hair."

Storage Houses

Plank houses used only for storage were owned by wealthy families. In these, row upon row of food hung from the roof beams or was stored in lidded cedar boxes carefully arranged along the walls. Some people claim that during the winter, servants kept fires going in these food storage houses for as long as the provisions lasted. The verification for this information is in our legends; no one has seen such a house.

Wooden Food Caches

Many believe that wooden food caches (*anyuusim gan*) were in use before the Europeans reached the area, but since the cache is only useful if the base of each supporting pole is wrapped with metal a few feet above the ground to prevent animals from climbing into the cache, and since copper, the only metal used by us, was not available in large sheets before the Europeans arrived, there is some doubt that the *anyuusim gan* are ancient.

The typical cache had a peaked or shed roof of cedar shakes and walls of plank or log. Long strips of cedar bark applied over the roof's ridge point and reaching to the base of the peak served as rainproofing. Roofs such as these have been seen by all of today's middle-aged band members. The floor was made of peeled poles and was supported by four sturdy cedar legs, one at each corner, that raised the cache six to ten feet above the ground. If the cache were unusually high, a notched ladder was on hand for human visitors. The food caches were never locked; most had a wood door as protection against the elements. Wood caches were frequently located behind the villages and were always placed well above high water.

Dry Storage

The ceiling area in the family house was a jungle of swinging shelves and hanging storage bags and baskets for very dry foods, such as dried rhubarb, seaweed and hemlock bark cakes. The housewife who did not want her hanging shelves to come crashing down made her rope from alder, which mice do not chew.

Aging

Some foods, such as the delicacy *logwolan* (matured fish eggs), were buried in wooden boxes a foot or two below ground level and left there several months until ripe. The hole was dug beneath a sheltering evergreen so that a minimum of snow had to be scooped away in winter when the stored food was removed from this natural deepfreeze.

Oolichan Grease as a Preservative

Oolichan grease served as a food preservative. Crabapples and various firm berries were coated with the grease and set in a cool place, in wooden boxes, until needed. The grease kept the air away from the food and thus slowed decay.

Birch Bark

Birch bark is important in food preservation. Our experienced woodsmen point out that if the bark is left on a fallen birch tree, the wood rots; this does not happen with any other species of tree. They believe that the rot occurs because birch bark, being watertight and airtight, "overseals" the fallen tree. We made good use of this characteristic of birch, which was the aluminum foil of our grandfathers.

When our people stored dry-smoked fish they put a layer of birch bark between each fish "so that if one fish rots the next won't spoil too." An excavation beside a very ancient fishing hole (three or four thousand years old) unearthed neat piles of good-sized birch bark squares, presumably stacked and ready to use in the food holes, storage boxes and ovens.

A recent excavation of the base of a totem pole, which had been raised between 1850 and 1860, uncovered a large birch bark food package which had contained berries. Only the seeds remained after 120 years,

Opposite: Last of the old food caches, formerly at Kispiox, installed at 'Ksan in 1975

Birch bark squares, ready for use in wrapping food for storage

but we estimate that the berries would have remained edible for several decades.

We have found in former food storage holes—holes that have not been used for at least sixty years— skeletons of whole fish in neat, birch bark cases. No meat remains today, but it is obvious that the fish had been wrapped and placed in the earth in order to preserve it.

Although many methods of preservation were used, almost all of our foods were smoked and dried before being stored for future use.

2

The Food We Ate

FISH WAS THE BASIC item among the foods we smoked and stored. Our abundant rivers and lakes kept us well supplied. Fish was served three times a day, at every meal. The fish might be one of the six varieties of salmon (we consider the steelhead a salmon) or trout (including the char, Dolly Varden) or, if things were really tough, the bony Rocky Mountain whitefish. With a little effort we could get oolichans and their rich grease from our neighbours, the Nass River people. We traded with the Coast people for all types of shellfish, particularly clams. We ignored eels, lampreys, freshwater shrimp, and scorned the bullhead.

Among the fish and fish parts that rank low on our edible food list are humpback salmon, dog salmon and fish offal, but fish hearts, eggs and sperm are eaten.

Except for the bones, we ate every part of the fish, including the head, the eyes and the offal. We wasted nothing edible, and we took extreme care to burn the fish bones, or to reassemble each fish and return it to the water so that the fish could reincarnate and come to us again.

The busiest time of the year was when the fish were running, because survival might depend on the amount of fish we could store. All the able-bodied people took part. The men did most of the great barrel trap (*moohl*) construction and setting. They speared the fish and manipulated the big dip nets. They manned the canoes in front of the fish weirs (*t'in*).

The women and children packed the fish to the smokehouse area, cleaned them, smoked or cooked them in various ways, then stored them away for the winter.

The fish are transported to the smokehouse area— perhaps in coarsely woven fish-pack baskets made of bark, roots or small branches, perhaps tied on a branch—then sorted and prepared for immediate consumption or for smoking.

The next step is to clean the fish with leaves and scrapers. "Fern, fireweed or peavine leaves were placed under the fish—a sort of disposable paper towel. These soiled leaves were never left to make a mess but were burned or thrown in the river. No discarded matter was ever left around. Peavine leaves were the best cleaners."

Some of our elders still follow many of these practices.

Fish for immediate consumption is boiled, barbecued, roasted or baked. We have already discussed boiling procedures (page 15). They are essentially the same for all foods. Our files tell of bygone days when

Spearing salmon

sometimes undressed salmon were placed upright in cooking boxes and boiled whole. This method was used especially with the jack spring, the first run of each year.

Another boiling technique used today as well as in ancient times is to take smallish pieces of dressed fresh fish and boil them gently just long enough to cook them through. Our word for this, *hagul jam*, which is translated "slow boil," is an accurate description of the method. Other boiled fish dishes are described in Section 3.

Barbecuing

Barbecuing a whole, undressed fish

If we are talking about cooking fish by our grandfathers' open fire method, barbecuing and roasting have the same meaning. But because today roasting and baking mean the same, since they usually refer to cooking in the oven of a cookstove, we will avoid confusion by using the word barbecue to indicate cooking on an open fire.

To barbecue whole, undressed fish (*bii'yan*), a stake (*anyoo*) of spruce or dry willow is threaded through the fish from head to tail in such a way that it weaves over and under the rib bones, close to the backbone. Small wooden skewers (*xhlaxws*) may be inserted through the fish at right angles to the stake. These skewers, and the stake through the ribs, keep the fish firmly in place during the cooking procedure. The other end of the stake is driven into the ground at such an angle that the fish is held over the fire, as illustrated. The stake is turned frequently to ensure even cooking. Red cedar is prefered for the skewers, but any wood that will not leave a sour taste may be used.

Because the *xhlaxws* are inserted through the fish at regular intervals, they serve as useful guides when dividing the fish into servings. So the word *xhlaxws* is the name given to a serving of fish, which is as large as the distance from one skewer to the next. The ceremonial serving of the first spring salmon was also called the *xhlaxws*.

Yoos Hon

Fresh fish may be dressed (including the removal of the heads), cut lengthwise into two or more long pieces and barbecued in the same manner. The skewers are even more important in this case because they keep the fish firm and rigid while it cooks; "You don't want it to curl up like birch bark." The skewers are imbedded in the meat and do not show during the cooking. They are removed before the fish is eaten.

How to barbecue a whole, filleted fish

A careful cook stands ready to catch the juices in a dish and bastes the fish with this liquid. Small holes may be made over the entire surface of the cooking fish with a sharp bone or wooden skewer. The juices are then poured into these holes, adding flavour and moisture to the final product. The pan used today to catch the juice is metal, but our grandfathers used utensils fabricated from wood, bark, roots, horn, bone and even stone.

Cooking Fish Heads

Whole fresh fish heads or parts of the heads are cooked in many ways. The "cheek" meat is particularly tasty and for that reason is occasionally set aside for some favoured person, but more often it is eaten as part of the head.

A dish using fish heads—which must be fresh—is described this way: "One day grandfather made a rack (*gan geeluxw*) to cook fish heads on. He used long thin sticks; about ten by eight feet was the size of the rack. He tied these sticks together with cedar bark and made nice legs for it. Grandfather used to go out and get some cedar bark, big wide ones. He would cut the tree down, then he cut the limbs off and cut the tree up about eight to ten feet long and then chopped the bark off. He would use

Barbecuing Spring salmon heads
Opposite: Cleaning fish on a bed of leaves

this bark for a covering on these heads while they cooked. It tasted very good when these fish heads were cooked over the open fire and smoke got on them. It's different. I used to watch this rack so that it did not burn. Grandfather put a net on the end of the stick for me with a pail of water beside me. If the legs started to burn, I would dunk the net into the water and wet the legs down. I was real good at watching and looking after these heads. When grandmother opened or took the covering off this rack of heads, then we would eat."

Another taped description says this about heads:

"They baked the [fresh] fish heads. If they're too full, and can't eat it all, they carefully peel off the skin from the head. They leave in the bones — the bones are really greasy and they could suck on them. They spread out the cooked fish head flat, with the *do'o* [cheek] in it still. They put a cedar bark string through the eye-holes and hang a whole string of them on the rack at the side of the smokehouse — not right close to the fire — on the side walls, too, sometimes. Really good for a sick person, too, they said, because that's where the really salmon strength is — in his head."

The illustration shows fish heads being cooked on a stake — another very tasty dish. In Section 3 we will tell you more about cooking fresh fish heads and other parts of the fish.

Drying Fish

Although our ancestors ate a fair amount of fresh fish, they ate at least twenty times as much smoked fish. The salting process which the Europeans introduced to our people in the nineteenth century changed our habits considerably, and modern deepfreezers and canning have changed them even more. The process of dry smoking fish was the most common one in pre-deepfreeze days, because with this method the fish kept indefinitely. Today, only about ten per cent of the fish that reaches the smokehouse is dry smoked; the other seventy-five per cent is half smoked to give it flavour and texture; then it is either canned or deep-frozen.

These days, in every Gitksan village when the salmon are running wherever you turn your eyes you can see smoke billowing out from little pioneer-style sheds. Your first reaction may be to sound the fire alarm, but there is no need: those smoking shacks are today's version of the great old smokehouses. The originals have vanished.

The fish-smoking technique has not vanished, though; it has continued essentially unchanged through generations of grandmothers. The tools have changed — sharp steel replaces knives of bone, tooth, shell

or stone—and fires are lit by matches, not by rubbing sticks together. But the smoking method remains the same.

We have already described the smokehouse organization in general; the next pages describe fish smoking in particular and one woman's method in detail.

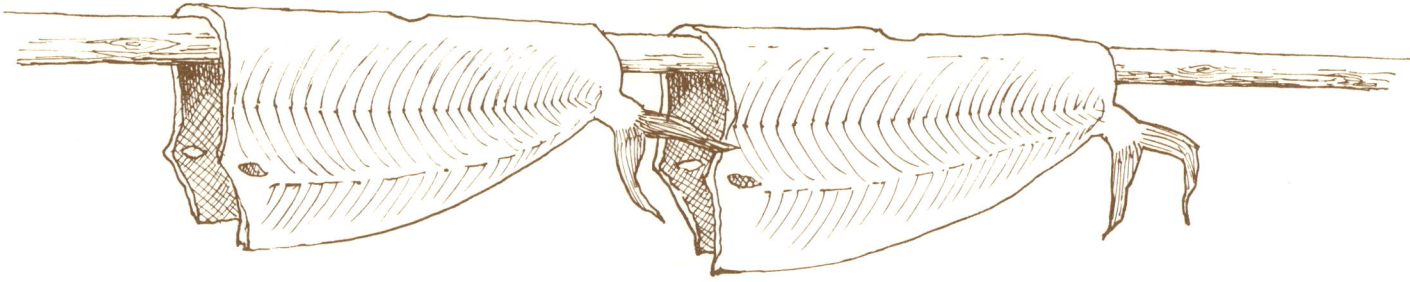

Fish hung to dry—horizontally (*above*) and (*opposite*) vertically. Note the filleting board in the foreground of the photograph

Smoking Fish

"The woman who makes good fish [i.e., smokes fish well] has to be a hard worker, very clean. She's up early and to bed late. If she's not actually preparing fish for the smokehouse, she's watching those fish already in the smokehouse, seeing that no flies get at the fish; tending the tiny, smoke-making fires; cleaning off any specks of soot; moving the fish again and again to see that they dry evenly and do not sour. She's got to be patient. If you're in a hurry nothing will be done right."

As each fish arrives at the smokehouse (*wilp sa hon*), the fish-maker puts it in a shady place until she can work on it, for fish sunburn easily. She may soak the fish awhile in water, if she believes that soaking makes the meat more tender. More likely she cleans it, removes its head, and hangs the fish in the smokehouse overnight, sometimes as long as a day and a half. Fish at this stage is called *pt'ikxw*. In bygone days she "wouldn't dare use water" to clean her fish, and even today little water is used, none after the smoking starts.

The fish is hung until it is dry and there is no slime left. Proper hanging tenderizes the fish, just as proper hanging tenderizes meat. Usually she puts a stick through the tail and hangs the fish vertically. The illustration shows a horizontal method as well. The fish-maker is very particular about the amount of heat at the *pt'ikxw* stage. If by some mischance the fish gets too hot, she invites everyone nearby to a little feast, *xmihl,* and the overheated fish is eaten or given away for quick use. Overheated fish cannot be smoked successfully and will not keep.

"If too much heat rises from the fires in the smokehouse the fish they drop off the *wit* [racks]. Then they can't smoke it, so they have to use it

Opposite: Filleting fish. *Right:* Fish hung for smoking

right away. They cook it up." Here, the informant paused, cupped her hands and raised them to her mouth to magnify the sound. Then, as though calling to someone, she continues, " '<u>G</u>ala sim hoo <u>x</u>mihlsm! Come eat the burned fish.' Then they all come and eat the fish that's too hot."

Next she takes the fish down and wipes it carefully with leaves—but never with water—to clean off any dirt or soot. (Today she uses a dry cloth.)

Now she takes the fish to a filleting board (*gan ts'al*) or a sturdy table, and cuts or fillets the fish so that the entire fish is spread out in one flat, even piece. She leaves in the backbone in all types of fish except the big spring salmon. She leaves the tail on. She fillets it so that the thickest slices are no more than three-eighths of an inch thick, "nice and thin so they would not sour." (A thicker slice would rot before it dried.)

You will notice in the illustrations that she works with the meat side up. She leaves on the skin as a backing for the fish, to give it extra strength and rigidity.

The fish-maker now returns the thinly sliced fish to the smokehouse and hangs it on cedar racks or crossbars (*wit*), not too far from the fires.

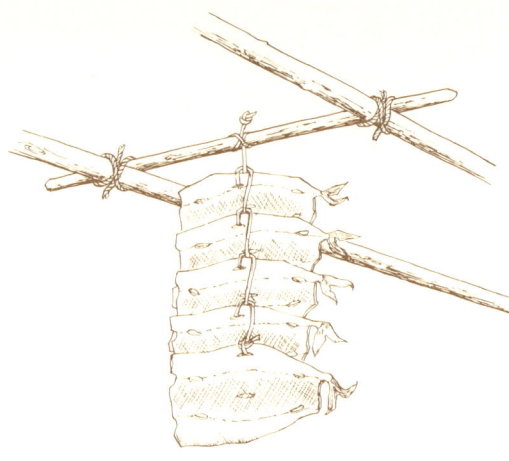

Fish in a bunch, hung for the final drying

When half dry, that is, when the moisture content is down approximately fifty per cent, she threads the fish on cedar "strings" and hangs it higher in the smokehouse (making room for unsmoked fish), where it is left until fully dry. She may then move it to the highest rafters until the smoking season is over, when it is taken down and stored away for the winter.

Some women move the fish to the upper level of the smokehouse only once during the smoking and that is when the fish is fully dry. They then tie the fish in bunches (_gahlgoosxw_)—each bunch usually contains forty fish—and move them to the highest rafters to give them a sort of "double dry," and to get them out of the way of fresher fish.

All salmon except dog salmon (_ganiis_) are smoked this way. "Dog salmon have to be soaked in cold water for about three days or they're hard as boards."

We Gitksan prefer lightly smoked, shiny fish. People in other areas enjoy a heavier, darker smoke (_gax lakws_).

If the fish-maker had wanted to half smoke some of the fish, she would have taken them out of the smokehouse after a couple of days or so, "the time depending on the humidity of the air and how strong she wants the smoked flavour to be."

The smoking of fish went on and on, as long as the fish continued to run. As many fish as it was humanly possible to smoke had to be smoked. Sometimes the work was exhausting, particularly if the fishing ground was far from our village and a long homeward journey with the finished product had to be faced, as witness this account:

"The work was long and tiresome. Grandfather took down the spring salmon and put thin sticks through them so that they could tie it on. The sticks were made just a little longer than the fish. These fish were all tied up together when we were about to move. [These sticks were bundled together for future use after they were taken off the fish.] The place... was quite a few miles from the village. Grandmother would pack a pile of forty fish, and I would pack about ten in my pile. Not all the fish were taken home right away. Some were stored in the smokehouse until a later date."

Not all the fishing and smoking was done in the summer. There was ice fishing in the winter:

"The snow was deep and Grandfather used to make snowshoes for me. He'd just bend a branch and put sticks across, then he'd work the inside in like the snowshoes are now. He used real cow hide or beef hide to fill it in and I'd use them when Grandmother and I went fishing through the ice. We caught lots and lots of fish. Even the dogs packed some on their backs, and Grandmother would clean them and slice them up and hang them up to dry. Every day we went fishing through the ice—there was a lot of fish at that time—early in the spring, around March or April; then we came home here [Kispiox]. Our sled was just filled with dried steelhead."

Fish Strips

Some parts of the fish require special attention.

When a fish is filleted, strips of fish meat are pared or sliced off to an even thinness for the smokehouse—"unless a big salmon is thinned down it rots before it dries." These parings or strips (*huxws* or *k'ay yuxws*) are occasionally set out on rocks, mats or boards to dry in the open. They must be turned repeatedly until dry. Some people put hanging racks outside for them. These very thin slices dry quickly. People who do not like the smoke flavour enjoy fish made this way. (We have controversial material in our files concerning air drying. Some feel it is unreliable because sun burns fish. Others are certain the old people air dried fish constantly.)

Because of their varying shapes and sizes, parings and strips are not the easiest things to hang in a smokehouse so wooden skewers sometimes are inserted to hold the meat together while it dries, several pieces being strung on one small rod to save space. These parings are never hung directly over the fire. The smallest ones usually go right into the soup pot —a kind of fish stew—and are eaten while fresh; the longer ones go to the smokehouse to make fish strips.

Good fish-makers roll the dried strips in neat oblong bundles about six to eight inches long by two inches wide and two inches deep, then tie them with one of the many kinds of Indian twine. *Huxws* are on our preferred dining list; they are all meat and no bone. We eat them just as they are or toast them and dip them into oolichan grease where they sizzle invitingly. The oil in the strips oozes out to the surface during the toasting and bastes them as they heat. *Huxws* are excellent food—"the most," our elders say, laughing as they use the modern slang.

Ts'okxw

"Very special" is how we rate the *ts'okxw*: the centre of the fish's belly. When we clean a fish and get it ready to smoke, we often cut a narrow strip off either side of the belly, where the two fins are, and soak the strips in salted water before putting them through the smokehouse routine. They are exceptionally rich in fat as well as being free of bones, and make fine eating.

The technique of soaking in salted water has obviously come about since contact with white people, who introduced salt.

Fish Eggs

Fish eggs (*am sk'iikx*), because of their small size and slippery texture, cannot be treated like the fillets. They are often dried for a while in the sun, to remove excess moisture, then hung in clusters on the walls of the smokehouse. We sometimes hang them over the rails in the smokehouse just as they come from the fish. They have concentrated food value. Our grandmothers were more likely to age them and make them into one of two now rare delicacies—*logwolan* and *'lana t'im ges*.

Logwolan is made by taking fresh fish eggs (or sometimes smoked eggs), wrapping them in birch bark, placing them in a cedar box and burying them in the ground until the mixture is ripened, like a good cheese. This could take a week or many weeks, depending on the temperature. Most cooks liked to save *logwolan* for the winter feasts and for emergency rations.

'Lana t'im ges is a mixture of fish eggs and raw meat from fish heads, treated in the same way as *logwolan*.

"They just mix up the heads with the eggs 'n wrap the whole bunch in birch bark and put them in the ground. The warmer it is the faster it's ready, I guess. I'm not sure how long it was before they could serve it but I think they always kept it for the wintertime because it was something that would keep well in the earth cellars. They said that fish eggs had lots of nourishment and a very small piece would keep a man going quite a long time."

"They only use sockeye for this because sockeye're small—they store them away raw.... My [former] husband remembers...his dad was sick and didn't eat for a week—he asked his mum to take out the eggs and head from the [earth] cellar. He ate them and next day he wasn't sick any more!"

The bent wooden box in which both of the delicacies were placed was often buried under the boughs of an evergreen tree, where the snow would not be too deep, thus making winter access comparatively easy. The box was covered with a layer of hemlock boughs or other protective greenery before the hole was filled with earth.

Both *logwolan* and *'lana t'im ges* were usually eaten raw, just as cheese is today. They could be a great boon in the spring when food supplies were running low. Both were so nutritious that people could survive on them and they often saved our ancestors' lives when the spring salmon run was late.

One informant told us: "I remember some wee, tiny little bunches of dried eggs—I'm not sure from what kinda fish they come—but my grandad used 'em on the trapline. A guy could put that little bunch in his cheek and keep it there like snoose almost about all day, an' he'd never miss his grub, an' never get hungry."

Logwolan and *'lana t'im ges* can be eaten with or without oolichan grease, cooked or uncooked. In recent times, people have occasionally been poisoned by these mixtures if they were stored in tin cans, but "nobody was poisoned in the ancient days when birch bark envelopes held the fish."

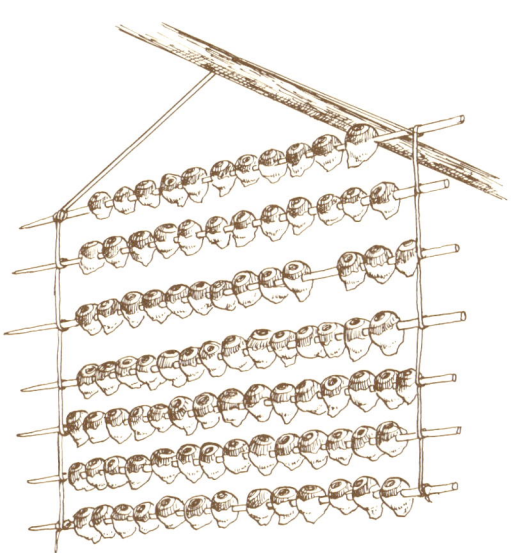

Fish eyes, skewered and hung in the smokehouse

Fish Eyes

Fish eyes (*ts'a'a*) are another delicacy requiring special preparatory techniques. Eyes are usually smoked by skewering them on thin rods eight to ten inches long and one-eighth inch in diameter. The filled rods are tied together to form small racks, which look like miniature venetian blinds, and hung in the smokehouse to dry.

Geekx

The waxy substance (*geekx*), found in the "nose" of a cooked fish head, is always eaten right away, never smoked or preserved. "It's good but not considered extra special."

Smoked Heads

Fish heads get special treatment because they cannot be filleted out like the body of the fish. Before smoking, fish heads are baked; then the eyes and cheeks are taken out, as well as the *geekx* just mentioned. When removing the *geekx* we make a cut through the lower lip of the fish, which makes it possible to open out the baked head. We allow the head to dry and then we tie strings from one head to another and loop the strings over drying rails.

Backbones

Spring salmon backbones are also smoked. "We simply double the bone over until it cracks but does not split apart, then hang it over a rack to smoke."

"The bits of meat that are close to the bone are the tastiest."

T'ul

We prize the triangular piece at the neck of the fish, called *t'ul*. When salting became known as a method of food preservation, the *t'ul* were often salted down separately in their own little barrel.

Oolichan

Besides taking the larger fish that our rivers and lakes provided, many of our people made an annual trip to the lower Nass River, chiefly to obtain the tiny oolichan, sometimes called the candle fish. The oolichan are extremely rich in oil, and no food outranked them in prestige or food value. We still value them highly, calling them "the little friend to all the world."

The preparation of the oolichan is a specialty of the Niska of the Nass, and we traded their oolichan for prepared dried fish, meat, tanned hides, soapberries, etc. Now we drive to the Nass to bring home fresh and smoked oolichan and oolichan grease.

For more about this delicacy, see page 89.

Other Foods from the Sea

Clams, abalone, halibut, red snapper, seaweed and other sea delicacies were also obtained through trade.

Whatever the species, however cooked or prepared, fish appeared on our eating mats every day, often at every meal. It was our year-round basic diet. To quote from our files, "The Stikine depending on meat, we depended on fish."

Meat & Fowl

NEXT TO FISH, our most important food was furnished by the animals and birds which abounded in our area in ancient times. The animals we eat are mountain goat, caribou, deer, porcupine, beaver, groundhog, lynx and rabbit. Sometimes eaten but less popular are bear, muskrat, wolverine and squirrel. Very few people eat grizzly bear. There are also many animals that we do not eat, such as marten, fox, wolf, mink, coyote, otter, weasel, rat or mouse, though most of these are taken for their fur. The birds we eat are grouse, goose, duck, ptarmigan, swan and sometimes seagull; we do not eat owls, ravens, crows, eagles or loons. Insects, frogs, toads, lizards and reptiles are not eaten, nor are worms.

The animals understood that our ancestors had to kill them for food. Out of respect for the animal's sacrifice, we took great care that no usable part of the animal was wasted and that unused parts were burned or placed out of the way of predators and dogs. Everyone made absolutely certain that animal blood did not spill on the ground and remain there.

In the case of beaver, all the bones were thrown back into the river or pond. If a beaver pond was empty, the bones were thrown back into it so that the beaver would eventually inhabit it again. One informant said: "When a beaver is gutted, the blood is covered up well so that dogs can't lick any from the ground." The old people believed that if a dog were to get some of the beaver blood, the beaver trap would make a peculiar noise when it was set, like a dog gnawing a bone. This noise would warn the beaver, and the trapper would go hungry.

There are no restrictions against eating the animal that is your crest, but most elders state that if a medicine man had a bird or animal for his talisman (*aatk'yasxw*—the symbol and embodiment of his curing power) he did not eat that creature.

There were restrictions concerning the eating of certain meats at certain times and by certain people. Young girls during their puberty seclusion were forbidden fresh meat, as were all women during their menstrual periods. "If they ate fresh meat their family would have bad luck in everything they did." Young boys were forbidden to eat certain parts of the animals, such as the head and legs of the bear. Pregnant women faced many dietary restrictions, most of them regarding fresh meat. "Even today we are very careful about giving away meat—we

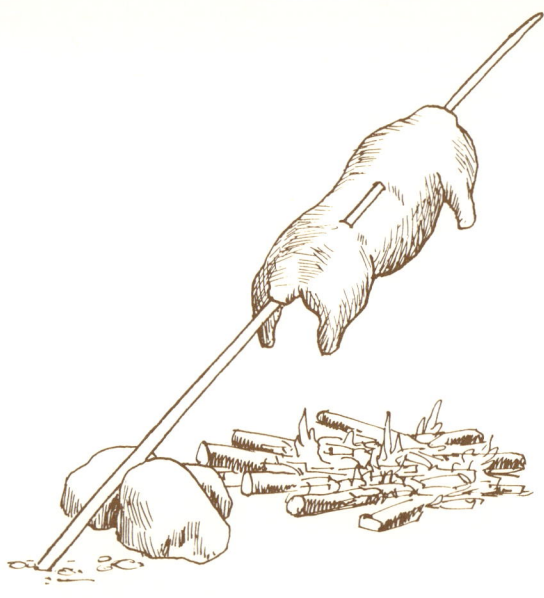

One way of cooking a beaver

don't want to spoil our hunting season by giving fresh meat to a woman who shouldn't eat it."

The preferred meat of our people was beaver. Beaver was valued so highly that it was forbidden to feed it to the dogs. Porcupine and groundhog were the ancient equivalent of pork chops. Fresh meat was a great treat because without refrigerators it would not keep. To prevent the fresh meat from rotting we usually smoked our kills as quickly as we could.

Cooking & Smoking

As with fish, meat and fowl are eaten freshly cooked, half dried or fully dried. When the meat of small animals or birds was to be smoked and dried, the whole animal was boned and opened out like a blanket, the intestines were removed, and the carcass was hung in the smokehouse.

Birds were first put in the fire to burn off the feathers, then cleaned, spread out as flat as possible and smoked whole. They are usually eaten immediately. Here is an interesting account:

"My dad told me about how they baked grouse on the trail. They'd coat the bird with mud, a thick coat... covering his feathers and all—leaving the guts in. They'd put the mud-covered bird in the hot coals; when the mud was baked hard, the bird was baked too, and they'd take it out of the fire and crack open the mud. The feathers would stay in the mud and there would be the bird, plucked, cooked, and ready to feast on."

Many still bone out the animals in the old style, keeping all the meat in one big piece like a blanket. Here is one lady's slightly edited description of drying a beaver:

"When I get the animal it's already skinned and gutted, but the head's on. You slit the flesh along each arm, one at a time, and cut the meat back from the bone. Then you make a slit at the front from where the animal was gutted up to the neck. You cut the meat back from each rib, keeping it in one unbroken piece, except for the slit down the centre of the front. You turn the animal over and do the same at the back. Then the head and all the bones lift out together... they stick together [and] I bury the bones....

"When I hang it in the smokehouse I put it over two hanging rails, side by side, but eight or ten inches apart. This spreads the beaver so it will dry evenly.

Above: Another method of cooking beaver over an open fire. *Below:* A beaver drying in the smokehouse

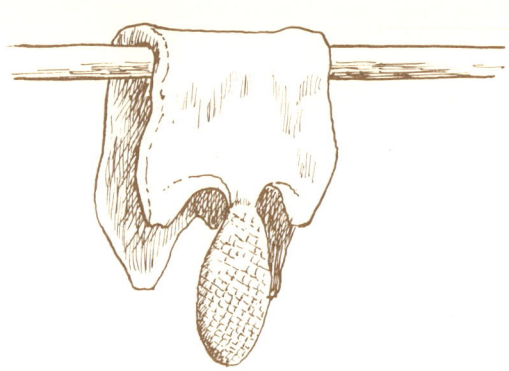

A second way of hanging a beaver for smoking

"I was advised to always build a big fire when I hung a beaver. Beavers are very fat, so you have to burn that fat off. It drips off and burns away in the fire. This also sears the meat, seals it and gives it good flavour, like meat that's nicely browned in a hot oven today. [The fat has a strong taste.] Then I put down the fire and go ahead with the drying. I move it [the beaver] often, just like the fish. You have to make sure it dries evenly and right through. I turn it every which way all the time."

Another lady recently smoked a mountain goat this way, though bigger animals are usually handled differently.

Most people now butcher wild animals in the same way that a cow is butchered. "But without saws or sharp knives our ancestors found it easier to lift the backbone out of the animals from the back, breaking through the tissues that hold the ribs to the backbone; they'd leave the animal a day or two so it would cut easier."

We smoke the ribs with the meat on them. The thicker, meatier parts are thinned or filleted into pieces about three quarters of an inch thick and hung in the smokehouse in the same way that we hang the fish strips.

Another informant gave us this description of smoking:

"Porcupines give us a little extra trouble when it comes to preparing them to eat because of the quills. The ladies often plucked out the quills for embroidery, but if they did not save the quills for decoration, they put the porcupine in a good hot fire and burned off the quills which form a white crust that lifts off easy. Porcupine is worth the extra trouble of removing the quills because the meat's really tender and has a good flavour."

"Granny used to boil a porcupine and she'd save me the legs to eat. Boy! it was good—I like it and still do. Grace often used to sit and watch me because she couldn't eat any while she had her monthly—about ten days after it was over, then she could eat meat."

Meats were usually smoked and dried on the hunting ground. Small temporary smokehouses were built for that purpose. Special pack boards were made on which the smoked meat was carried home by man, woman, child and dog.

Most small animals were eaten unsmoked unless they were very so numerous that all of them could not be eaten fresh. Here is an account of how one person's grandmother prepared fresh meat:

"When we got back from trapping she would skin the lynx and stretch it, and she would cook up the meat for all of us to eat. The meat was light in colour and it tasted like rabbit meat. We all liked it. But now I don't think I could eat it somehow, I don't feel right about it any more.

We do not eat fish, meat or fowl raw. The old people made one exception: the contents of the stomach of a caribou, which they ate warm, if possible immediately after killing the animal. In the wintertime this was the way they got vitamins and carbohydrates—predigested by the caribou.

In our recipe section we give a few cooking hints for meat, fish and fowl dishes.

Cooking Grease

While discussing fish, fowl and meats we must not forget the fats, greases and oils that these creatures provide.

Anyone who has heard our legends knows that a nice piece of fat was a highly prized commodity. What does our little Mouse Lady, Uu'n Jiits, ask in payment for her lifesaving advice? A little piece of fat. And every Gitksan knows how Weget once taunted Stump with the tempting treasure—a chunk of hot, crispy fat. (Weget is the Gitksan equivalent of Raven, the trickster-transformer of the Pacific Northwest Indians.)

Bears, groundhogs, mountain goats and salmon contributed most of the fats and greases we used in cooking. In addition, the oolichan, or candle fish, not found in the Upper Skeena, "topped the grease list" of our nobility, with the result that our people made an annual expedition to the Nass River in quest of oolichan grease. We shall talk more about this later.

When we use the word grease we are describing what most English-speaking people would call oil. Oolichan grease usually refers to a substance that looks like a good vegetable oil and has the same consistency.

We used—and still use—a lot of grease, serving it on or with most of our dried foods. We often put a little bowl of grease on the eating mat and dipped the hot or cold dried food in it in the same way that potato chips are dunked in today's dips. Grease improved the dried food just as butter improves bread.

We used grease to add zest to foods. In fact, it was our major condiment before sugar, salt, pepper or spices came our way. Grease coated fresh, uncooked berries, dried fish or meat, succulent raw or cooked roots and greens—almost every food was, we felt, improved by the addition of a little grease, particularly oolichan grease.

We added unrendered fats, or coarse greases, in cake form or in great chunks when we boiled dried meats and fish. This fat helped reconstitute the bone-dry food, making it softer and more palatable.

Our use of grease as a preservative has already been discussed, and as you read on you will see that grease is essential to certain fruit dishes.

Before cakes, candies and pastries were known to us, a hot, crisp morsel of grease was the richest, tastiest food we knew. All our middle-aged have happy recollections of crisp sheets of fat cooked over a fire, then divided and served "burning hot."

People who are middle-aged today remember their grandparents preparing as a treat a nice piece of toasted suet on the end of a stick, called *moosxan*. This word literally means "thumb chew" — and as one person said, "Maybe it was their popsicle!"

The hunter's survival kit was grease in one form or another. "He might pack along a bladder containing suet or a roll of mountain goat fat. A hunter could get along without any food but that suet or fat for quite a while."

The wise ones who healed our cuts and bruises told us to put clean, soft uncooked fat on torn skin and on burns.

Salmon Grease

We extracted a rich, all-purpose grease from salmon heads or whole fresh fish. This we served largely with dried fish and on occasion as a condiment for berries, roots or bulbs. "It refines to a nice, thin oil, making it a good food preservative. As it comes from the salmon the oil is often pinkish, and even quite red, but the expert can make a clear, colourless grease with no taste of fish and no dark colour, mild enough to use with fruit."

Here is one man's account of the process, although not everyone agrees with his conclusion:

"To make this grease, we soak salmon heads (usually spring salmon heads) for several days in cold water until they are soft. Then we boil them and boil them until all the grease comes out and rises to the top of the boiling water. We skim this grease off. We may have to repeat this several times to get a clear, colourless, mild grease. Not very many people do this today.

"The humpback salmon was used almost exclusively for grease. Great quantities of the fish were allowed to mature for a few days until soft. Then the grease was rendered out by boiling, just the same as with the salmon heads.

"When it's properly done, this grease is better than oolichan grease, nice flavour, no taste at all."

Berries & Fruit

EARLIER WE DESCRIBED the happy spirit that prevails on a berry gathering expedition. Here is a verbatim account of one such expedition and of the berry drying technique that was a fine art with our grandparents. The lady who gave the account has made berry cakes within the last several years. Her account concerns the drying of huckleberries, but the method is much the same for all berries that are dried.

"In the month of September when the huckleberries are ripe, the housewives make plans to go berry picking. All in the house help prepare and gather food, such as fish and meats, and put them in boxes, enough to last a month or until the berries are picked and dried. Early in the morning they start off with the large Indian boxes and cedar and spruce root baskets. They reach the cabin in the mountains, called *wilp ha'nii jokx* [house for all the world], the place where the berries are dried. They start to pick the huckleberries. Who is the fastest picker is the one who fills the Indian box first. They bring them home to the cabin, *wilp ha'nii jokx*.

"When all the boxes are full, now how to cook them? They choose some giant cedar boxes and tie them with twisted cedar rope to prevent them from breaking. The ladies crush the berries first before they cook them. They remove the juice from the berries. [See *aksa maa'y,* page 94.] They place them in the large boxes they chose. They build a fire and gather stones and put them on the fire until the stones are red hot.

"They make tongs from a straight green willow tree about five feet long and four inches in diameter. They split the bottom end half way. They use tongs to lift the hot stones and drop them in the boxes with the crushed raw berries. The berries boil very fast. The red-hot stones make them boil. It doesn't take very long. Soon all the berries are cooked.

"They prepare the dryer. It's made just like a small fence. Four posts, about three feet high, hold several wooden racks made of red cedar, six feet long and eighteen inches wide.

"They prepare some skunk cabbage leaves. They cut off the stem on the back of the big leaves and slightly dip them in the fire or in the boiling water for few seconds to make them soft. They lay uncooked skunk cabbage leaves on the rack first, then the slightly cooked skunk cabbage leaves; then they pour some cooked berries on the rack and build the fire under the dryer, not too much fire under the dryer and not too little. The fire goes on and on.

Opposite page, top: Picking huckleberries. *Bottom:* Racks ready for berry drying. *Above:* Crushing the berries

Above: Boiling the crushed berries. *Opposite page, top:* Spreading the berries on a bed of leaves. (Here salmonberry leaves are being used instead of skunk cabbage leaves.) *Bottom:* Checking for doneness

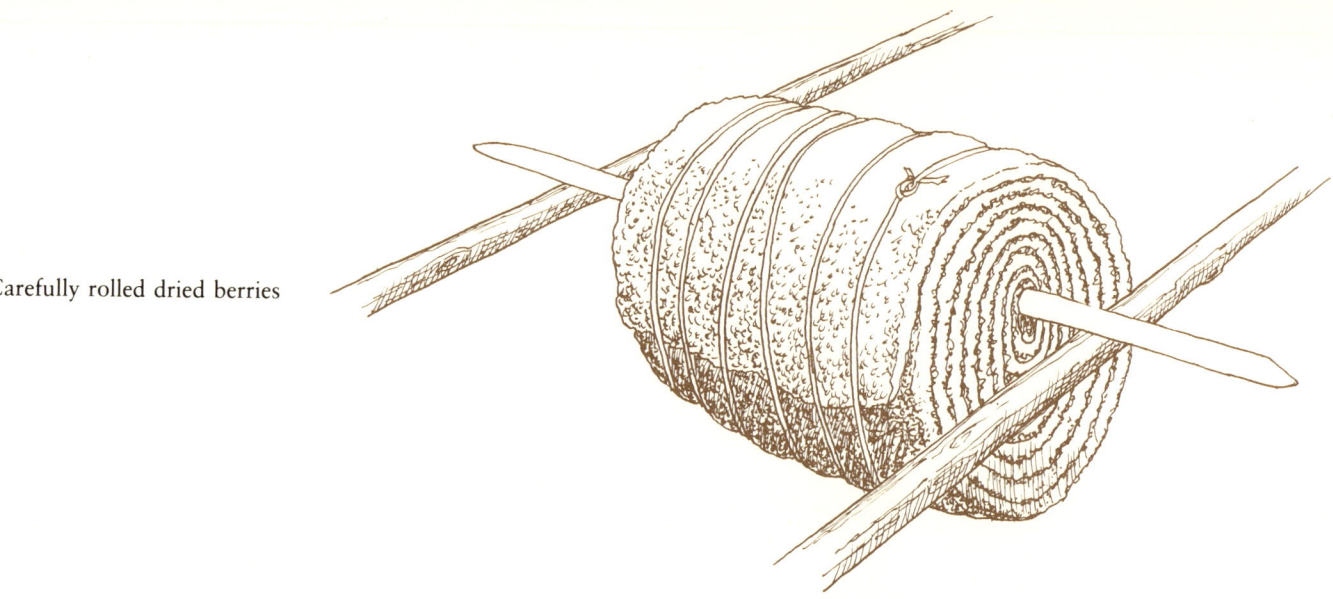

Carefully rolled dried berries

"The next day they check the berries with the palm of the hand. If the berries are sticky it is not time to turn them and they wait a little longer. When they will not stick to your hand they are ready to turn upside down. Take the raw skunk cabbage leaves and lay them on top of the half-dried berries, lay a spare wooden rack on top of the skunk cabbage leaves and it's ready to turn upside down. Two ladies do this. They hold the edge of the racks together, lift them and turn them over fast as they can.

"Now they remove the skunk cabbage leaves from the top of the berries and they shape the edge [of the berries to fit the rack].

"They keep the fire going on and on, every day. If the fire goes out, all the berries will taste sour.

"Now turn the berries upside down again. Don't use skunk cabbage this time. When the berries are completely dried, start to roll them in a big circle about twelve inches in diameter until you reach the end.

"Now take a stick, not too big, about the size of a broom stick, and thread this rod in all the rolled berries and stand [the rolls] in a warm place or hang them up near the roof until they are all completely dry.

"Then take them down and flatten out the rolls. Cut them and put them in the Indian boxes and take them home and store them in a nice clean, dry place."

Berry rolls are cut into cakes and we call them *k'ots maa'y*. The cake may be made bite size or big enough for several people. These pieces might be eaten plain, as would a dried apricot or peach, or they might be dipped in grease. The dry cakes are a handy food to take along when hunting or trapping.

Berry cakes vary in size, depending upon the size of the box in which they are to be stored. Some of these Indian boxes are giant sized, and the berry cakes that are to fit into them are cut into huge squares. The finished berry cake is from one-quarter to one-half inch thick.

The procedure of cutting long sheets of dried berries and placing them in boxes was done largely for trade. Just as often we carefully rolled the sheet, as the account describes, but left it in rolls.

"I remember, my mother was very particular the way she tied those rolls. They looked neat and nice. She took Indian twine and wound it around one end [of the roll] several times so it was tight and would not unwind. Then she wound the twine round and round the roll, moving closer to the other end of the roll each time she circled the roll. At the other end she tied the twine firm. This way the rolls would stay rolled. When she'd done this, she put a stick through the centre of the roll and she got someone to hang the rolls up high in the rafters of the house, where they'd stay dry."

It's important to keep rain off the drying berries. Consequently, if the berry patch is far from home, the drying racks are usually sheltered by the roof of the little berry drying house. Berries picked close-to home are dried in the fish drying house (*wilp sa hon*) if there is room.

Rolling the long flats of berries when they are taken off the drying racks is no simple job. "The ladies take great care. Work together. The rolls mustn't split. Sometimes they fill the cracks with the sticky sweet centre of the bunchberry [go goyp]. Skunk cabbage leaves are best for using on the berry racks but they're not in everybody's berry patch." Thimbleberry leaves and even ferns may be substituted. "It's safer to have many leaves (too thick a layer) than not enough. They don't want the berries to run through."

"Building the drying racks is a job for an expert, a real careful guy." The old racks we have in our museum at 'Ksan are beautifully made. The crossbars or slats are slender and absolutely even; a machine could not have done a more exact job. Every slat is the exact mate of its neighbour. The framework is equally well made. Each slat is bound to the frame with neat wrappings of split spruce roots.

"The uprights which support the racks and hold them over the smoke are the same length so that the berry rack is dead level. We don't want the berries to run to one end and make an uneven cake. The spread-out berries must be evenly spread so that the berries dry at the same rate all over."

Except for saskatoons, all berry drying followed this procedure. Because the dried saskatoons crack very easily, the cook often spread a layer of crushed bunchberries on top of the saskatoons before rolling them. "I always left quite a few leaves and stems with the berries that we were going to dry. This holds them together better. The roll doesn't crack."

There are four other berry preserving methods: the berries can be boiled and dried in the sun in wooden trays or on big leaves; uncooked berries can be set on mats to dry in the sun; they can be preserved in oolichan grease; or they can be boiled into a kind of sugarless jam, although the latter is no longer done. To boiled berries, bunchberries were often added as a thickener—our ancestors' Certo. "This [jam] doesn't keep long."

Today, berries are sun dried on canvas, heavy paper or other available modern materials that will keep them clean and away from the soil.

When the berries are fresh and ripe we eat great quantities of them. The older people still enjoy them shining with grease whereas the younger generation prefers sugar and cream. A traveller whose path leads him to a berry gathering group can expect to eat a healthy serving from the box of each picker. Failure to do so would be an insult to the picker, so a large group can present quite a challenge to a visitor's capacity.

Soapberries

The white people call our *is* berries by the name "soapberries" because, when whipped, the berries make a thick foam resembling stiffly beaten egg whites or soapsuds.

With the help of friends from the National Museum of Man, we are able to give you a fairly good photographic record of soapberry gathering—and eating.

The photograph shows a picker with her bent cedar box tied on her back by rope made of the inner bark of the red cedar. In her left hand she carries the special oblong cedar mat used for soapberry picking. It is doubled over and sewn on one side to form a sort of bin into which the berries fall as the picker knocks them from the branch with a stick (seen in our picker's right hand). The mat is called *ha'nii yats is,* which means "for hitting soapberries on top of."

When the boxes are full, the soapberries are ready for the next stage, perhaps for making the "instant dessert," *yal is* ("soapberries turned around and around"). If so, uncooked, fully ripe berries are squeezed by

Off to the berry patch. (The carrying strap or tumpline would often be worn across the forehead instead of the shoulders.)

Filling the box

Whipping the soapberries

A chief enjoying his dessert

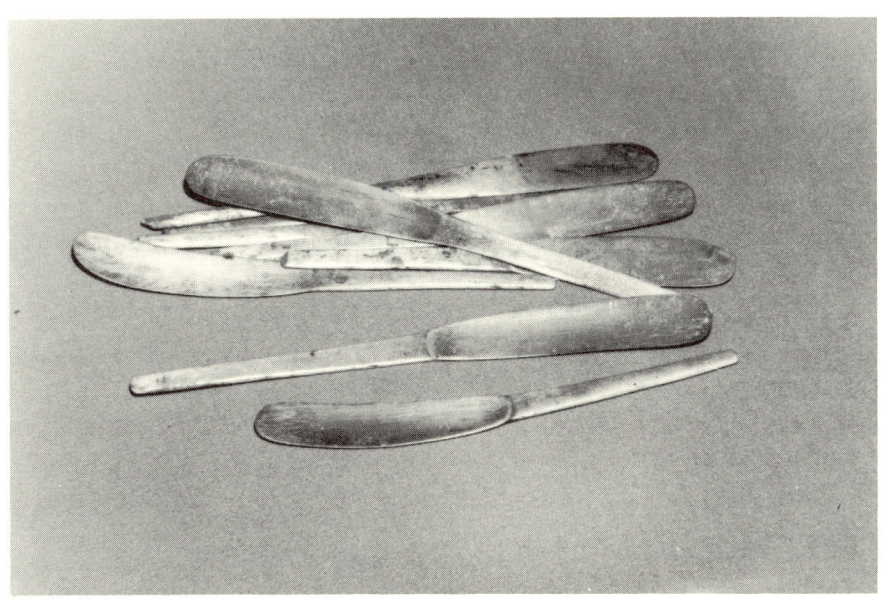

Cariboo-rib soapberry spoons

hand, the seeds discarded and a little water added. The mixture of berries and water is then whipped with the hand until the container is full of the thick creamy mixture. In ancient times no sugar was added; today we add lots of sugar, as the *yal is* is otherwise very bitter. Green berries whip as well as fully ripe berries, but most cooks prefer to cook the green ones before whipping them. Ripe berries whip into a delicate pink fluff with lots of eye appeal; the green berries make a chartreuse-coloured whip. The spectacular feature of this berry is the enormous quantity of whipped desert that can be made from a minimal quantity of fruit.

Yal is does not rank as a gourmet dessert. On the contrary, our files tell of slapstick games played with the mixture, games that sometimes ended with the chief wearing the container or bowl as a hat and most of the players spattered with some of the foamy mixture. (Our word *'niist* means to smear with soapberry foam.) When eating *yal is* people play the same kind of tricks with it that they do with bubble gum, pushing out the *yal is* and retracting it.

Special spoons are used for *yal is*. In our 'Ksan collection we have an unusual set of fourteen of these spoons, flat and unadorned, made from caribou ribs.

"*Yal is* is just right after very rich food. It makes your stomach feel better."

(A drawing of the soapberry—*Shepherdia canadensis* to the botanist—appears on page 73.)

Cedar bark basket, and another on the opposite page

All other berry species are picked by hand. Most pickers wear a small basket suspended from a rope that goes around the neck. The baskets are usually made of birch bark but some are woven from cedar bark. The neck rope slips through loops of skin inserted in opposite sides of the basket and suspends it, leaving both hands free to pick.

Most picking baskets are constructed with a lip around the top inside edge. When the basket is full, large, wide leaves are placed on top of the berries and small branches are inserted below the lip, reaching from one side of the basket to the other and crisscrossing each other at several places. In this way the sticks and leaves form a lid that keeps the berries from spilling. The smaller baskets are emptied into larger ones, or into bent wooden boxes.

Very small bent wooden boxes are also used by pickers. They too can be suspended from the neck to hang at waist height, or at whatever level is handy for the picker. These wooden boxes are often constructed so that when empty they can be stacked inside each other in sets of two, three or four; they can range in size from about ten inches square (for a little girl) to eighteen inches square, though such a large box would more

likely be used for a main storage box rather than a picking box, unless the picker were stronger than average.

The picked berries were taken to the "berry dry house" (*wilp ha'nii jokx*) located at the berry patch. "If there was no berry drying house, one was built right away in the form of a lean-to or A-frame—we had to make sure that the berries kept dry during the smoking or air drying process. These houses, which might also be used for meat smoking, were roughly constructed, sometimes of planks split from cedar but more often from whole logs, boughs and cedar bark. The men were happiest if they could haul in dry balsam logs from a burn, for balsam is light and once scorched does not decay quickly. If the patch was a big and reliable one, the berry drying racks were carefully stored inside the drying house from year to year. Berries could also be dried in any fish-smoking house that was nearby and not in use.

Today the houses are rarely used. Few people dry berries, for it is a time-consuming process and the end product is not very juicy. These days berries are brought home and canned or deep-frozen by modern methods.

Huckleberries

Our name for huckleberries, *sim maa'y,* means "the real, the true berry" which describes well our esteem for them. "They are the favourite for drying, retaining their fine flavour through the drying process, and they are easy to roll when dried. Also, they preserve well in grease. We can even keep them for quite a while by putting them away in a cool place in boxes without any preservative."

Saskatoons

Saskatoons (*gyam*), or serviceberries, grow everywhere, like the dandelions and thistles that the traders brought in. When drying saskatoons on the racks, some cooks add an extra layer of fresh crushed berries towards the end of the drying period. They claim that this prevents the berries from cracking when they are rolled. Others add the sticky substance that results from mashing bunchberries (*go goyp*).

Saskatoons and soapberries were dried in bite-size chunks for which we have the name *maa'y tsa*. They are the only varieties of berry used for this food. *Maa'y tsa* was usually eaten without being softened in water—"just a nice, chewy mouthful."

Saskatoons are also sun dried, "spread out on cedar mats which were shaken every now and then so that the berries dried all round." When dried, they resemble a tiny raisin.

Cranberries & Crab Apples

We have both high bush cranberries (*ts'idipxst*) and low bush cranberries (*'mii oot*). The high variety are good keepers and preserve well in grease without precooking.

Wild crab apples (*milkst*) are common. They are too hard to be made into cakes but "keep *perfectly* in grease." Some cooks boil them a minute or two to soften them a little before coating them with grease. Even without grease or preservative, crab apples keep for a long time in earth cellars. Big baskets and boxes of them were kept that way "right into the winter." It is interesting to note that today's professional fruit growers dip their apples in wax before marketing them. The wax does the same work that our grease did, but "the wax hasn't the flavour or food value of grease."

Huckleberry (*Vaccinium parviflorum*)

Saskatoon berry (*Amelanchier alnifolia*)

High bush cranberry (*Viburnum edule*)

Low bush cranberry (*Vaccinium vitis-idaea*)

Salmonberries

Salmonberries (*'mii k'ooxst*) are scarce in our area, but delicious when we do find them. They look something like a raspberry but are "kind of salmon egg colour" and are so juicy that they cannot be made into berry cakes, so are only eaten fresh.

Stonecrop

Also eaten fresh are the dark red berries that grow on low rock plants, two to five inches high. This is the common stonecrop sedum, *t'ip yeest,* found in abundance around Twin Lakes near Kispiox and at Moricetown, and you will read more about them on page 87 in the section on greens. If you drink water after eating these berries, they leave a "nice taste in your mouth."

Frogberries

Frogberries (*'mii ganaa'w*), or dewberries, grow on a plant six to seven inches high having a small maplelike leaf. "The berry is red and shiny and looks something like a raspberry but paler and with fewer bumps, maybe about four." They grow in shaded places in long grass or underbrush and are only eaten fresh, being too juicy to be made into cakes.

Blueberries

Blueberries (*'mii yahl*) dry well and can be preserved in grease. We have two varieties: the big grey berry that we mix with huckleberries if the huckleberry crop is scarce (they are mealy and not too tasty) and the smaller blueberries which grow close to the ground and are a favourite with all of us.

High Bush Blueberries

"High bush blueberries (*'mii gan*) grow, as you'd expect from their name, in high places along with huckleberries. If there's lots of huckleberries we don't bother to pick these greyish-blue berries because they are too seedy." These blueberries grow on thin shrubs about two feet high and are bigger than the blueberries that grow close to the ground. Some white people call them mountain berries or blue huckleberries. Sometimes we mix them with huckleberries when making berry cakes.

Salmonberry (*Rubus spectabilis*)

Stonecrop (*Sedum divergens*)

Frogberry (*Rubus chamaemorus*)

Blueberry (*Vaccinium ovalifolium*)

Elderberries

Elderberries (*loots'*) are very bitter. Today, most of our young people are unaware that we ever ate them. According to our informant (who knows of the process though she has never seen the "jam" made) elderberries were crushed and boiled, then poured into small boxes lined with birch bark. The cooked berries set into a kind of jam without the addition of pectin or sugar. (Only red elderberries, not the sweeter blue ones, grow in the land of 'Ksan.)

Indian Glads

Indian glads (*k'ots*), or false Solomon's seal, has a long, scented white blossom and a small, round leaf. The plant produces tiny red berries which are picked ripe in August and preserved with oolichan grease. They are not made into cakes but stored in boxes in cool places. One person said, "They were hard to gather so we served them only to chiefs." Another stated, "Its edible seeds were added later and mixed with the berries."

Bunchberries

Bunchberries (*go goyp*), or clusterberries, grow in clusters of four or five on a low plant which has a white flower in spring and "leaves that resemble a four-leaf clover. The berries are red outside with white insides that look something like a marshmallow." Clusterberries can be served by themselves but are more important as a thickener for other berries and "to make berry cakes stick together and not crack." Our informants have identified the berry from books as a miniature dogwood.

Bearberries

Bearberries, or kinnikinnick (*t'mii'it*), preserve well in grease. "Pick out the little ones if you intend to preserve them; the big ones have too big pits [seeds]. Some are just about all pit; they just use those with little pits." They grow close to the ground on a pretty evergreen plant with thick leaves which, some people say, could be used as tobacco. Some of them stay on the bushes through the winter. "These berries survive the winter, and if they escape the bears, are still edible in the spring and a great treat if you can come across some of them."

Red Elderberry (*Sambucus racemosa*)

Indian glads, or false Solomon's seal (*Smilacina amplexicaulus*)

Bunchberry (*Cornus canadensis*)

Bearberry, or kinnikinnick (*Arctostaphylos uva-ursi*)

This little berry is an important figure in one of our legends about Weget. The Trickster came upon a clump of bearberry. Hungry as usual, and cunning as ever, he decided to capture the berry. By dint of flattery he addressed it. "You remind me of tears on the cheeks of my favourite and most celebrated uncle." But the berry was not fooled. "Who doesn't know you, Weget?" it said, and rolled off the bush and hid in the safety of the woods. The little brown lines that may form on the berry are said to be the marks of Weget's uncle's tears.

Raspberries & Strawberries

Only one person has recorded information about raspberries (*naasikx*) or strawberries (*'mii gunt*). This reliable person claims that strawberries "were the prince of berries." We know that they are too juicy for the berry rack and therefore are always eaten fresh. An ancient village, northeast of what is now Terrace, was called "Place of Strawberry," which indicates that the berries grew in the area in distant times.

We have no record of raspberries having been used for any purpose whatsoever in ancient days, yet they grow like weeds here. They are too juicy for drying.

Thornberries

The thornberry (*snax*) found its way to our berry racks and food baskets, but it wasn't a favourite. It is a large, dark red—almost black—berry which grows on the hawthorn throughout the area. The fruit is dry and mealy and was eaten only if nothing else was available. One of our former villages was called by the Gitksan word for thornberry: "Place of *Snax*."

Pincherries & Chokecherries

Pincherries (*snaaw*) and chokecherries (*ts'ook'*) thrive here. We know that past generations ate them, but we have not been able to get any details. Neither is suitable for berry cakes. Our word for the chokecherry means that "it makes your mouth and throat so that nothing will slip on it." We use the same word when we sand an icy hill. This word accurately describes what chokecherries do to the mouth and throat: "Your mouth gets puckered and dry and the food won't slip down." Pincherries are tiny orange-red berries that are almost all pip. Today both pincherries and chokecherries are made into good jelly.

Thornberry (*Crataegus douglasii*)

Pincherry, or Western bitter cherry (*Rubus emarginata*)

Chokecherry (*Prunus virginiana*)

Soapberry (*Shepherdia canadensis*)

Rose Hips

Rose hips were known to be edible, for we have records of "jams" being made by mixing rose hips with other berries, but today we do not eat them. Botanists have told us that the berrylike seeds of the wild rose (*gale'e*) are full of Vitamin C. A satirical song mocks someone who overate rose hips and suffered an itching anus.

Gooseberries & Black Currants

Wild gooseberries (*dilawasa*) and black currants (*t'uuts'xwa maa'y*) are also on our uncertain list. We have no special information about them in our files. The older people believe that both grew here long ago.

Thimbleberries

Thimbleberries (*nisk'o'o*) are eaten fresh, usually mixed with other kinds of berries. They do not dry well or keep well when preserved in grease. By themselves, thimbleberries are dry and not very tasty.

Having described the berries that can be safely eaten, we will tell you some of the ways we serve them now and have served them in the past.

'Witsxw Maa'y

This means crushed (literally, squeezed) berries. "The fresh berry makes the tastiest dish" but dried berries can be used. They are soaked and then served, already having been crushed or squeezed. Here is one cook's way of serving *'witsxw maa'y:*

"Clean two quarts of fully ripe berries. Mash them or squeeze them. Add one cup of water and half a cup of sugar."

Dayks

This is a wintertime dessert since the recipe calls for snow. Snow, water and oolichan grease are whipped together until they form a thick creamy mixture similar to whipped cream. "Berries are stirred in—any small berries may be used. Crab apples or large, hard berries would not

Rosehips (*Rosa nutkana*)

Wild gooseberry, or swamp gooseberry (*Ribes lacustre*)

Black currant (*Ribes hudsonianum*)

Thimbleberry (*Rubus parviflorus*)

mix well; neither would very soft, juicy berries because they'd go to mush."

Hlayax

The combination of berries or fruit with oolichan grease but without snow we call *hlayax*. Crab apples, huckleberries, blueberries, cranberries and bearberries make good *hlayax*, especially if it is to be kept for any considerable length of time. Although these are not the only fruit used for *hlayax*, they are the most suitable because they are firm, not too juicy and thus have good keeping qualities (they keep their shape). Today we can use frozen berries for this dish.

"*Hlayax* was used by *si'moogit* [the chief] as a main course of feasts."

In the opinion of the old folk, any berry was improved by the addition of grease. In consequence they served even the freshest berries with a shining dressing of one of the more fluid types of grease. Before adding berries, the grease—usually oolichan—is mixed with a little water and beaten by hand until it is creamy. White, clear oolichan grease is our preference for both *dayks* and *hlayax*. The Nass River people prefer a stronger, darker grease, but we feel that strong grease kills the flavour of the fruit.

Hlayax is a rarity today, but many still make it on occasions and many more have eaten it. One of our friends has some *hlayax* in her deepfreeze — a "new" dish for her grandchildren.

Nisk'o'o

Nisk'o'o (thimbleberry—leaf or berry) is a children's dessert or snack. Freshly cooked or crushed berries are put into a thimbleberry leaf which has been folded to form a cone-shaped holder. The children suck the berries out of the small end of the cone or nibble them off the top.

Tubers, Bulbs, Roots, Bark & Greens

BEFORE THE DAYS of grocery stores, tubers, bulbs, roots, bark and greens also provided vital sources of food. Many of these native plants are still eaten by our people, and we describe some of the more interesting ones.

Wild Rice

One edible bulb is <u>gasx</u>, a name which we translate as "wild rice." This plant (the chocolate lily) grows in open flats; today it grows abundantly where hay has been cut. It also grows above timber line in the mountains. <u>Gasx</u> has a small, round leaf and deep maroon-coloured flowers which bloom in May. The plant grows to about two feet in height, and the flowers have an unpleasant odour.

The bulbs are gathered in June before they become woody. They are peeled to release the kernels which are washed in cold water, boiled and served with oolichan grease. Today they are most often served with sugar. Sometimes the kernels were toasted and served with hemlock sapwood. They can also be sun dried, then stored in wooden boxes or baskets.

Wild rice has an unusual, strong flavour and leaves an unpleasant aftertaste. This accounts for its Gitksan name which means "unpleasant." It is definitely an acquired taste. Hardly anybody eats our wild rice today, but most of our elders tasted it in their younger days and the generation before theirs considered it to be a great treat.

When the bulbs are overripe and dry, children enjoy popping them because the seeds burst out with a loud "crack" and explode all over the place.

A<u>x</u>

A<u>x</u>, the bulblet fern, grows in clearings near or on mountains. It has fernlike leaves and forms a dark brown "root," two to six inches long, which we eat. The root looks something like a woody sweet potato, tastes something like one and has much the same texture and colour when cooked.

A<u>x</u> can be gathered in either spring or fall. Some claim to have cleared away snow and dug up the root in the very late fall or early winter. It is not edible during the summer months, just as a seed potato in the ground

Gitksan wild rice: the chocolate lily (*Fritillaria camchatcensis*)

is not edible once it starts to produce more potatoes. In spring the "short, curly brownish-green stem sticks out of the ground to show where the *ax* is hiding."

Ax is dug by both men and women. The root is only two or three inches below the ground but the soil it grows in is hard; "it's tough to dig."

"*Ax* is black when you dig it, orange when you cook it, like a red turnip. Most times they bake it right where they dig it. They bake it with the skin right on, in the pits. They take it home in the big wooden boxes. It grows not very deep, but in *hard* ground."

"They say it's hard to pick out of the ground. One elderly lady said to my mum, 'You got the great big *ax* because your great big dad's hands is strong.'"

Books about plants say that *ax* is rare, but it is very plentiful around Kuldo, a deserted Gitksan village about ninety miles north of the present town of Hazelton, on the Skeena River. *Ax* grows close to several modern Gitksan villages, too. One ex-Kuldo man remembered gathering quantities of *ax* with his mother. They left most of their pickings in a dry shed and returned for them when other food supplies ran out. His mother simply "covered it with brush and leaves to keep off the snow and left it in the trapping cabin." Kuldo people were said to have the best *ax*, larger and of better flavour than elsewhere. Because they ate such quantities of the root, teasing songs have been written about their *ax* consumption.

Ax, the bulblet fern (*Cystopteris bulbifera*)

Ax is never eaten raw. It may be baked overnight in ovens dug into the ground. In modern times it has been canned. After the *ax* is cooked, it is peeled in the same way as a banana and served as a dessert with oolichan grease and, today, sugar. Here is a description of the baking of *ax*, given to us by a former Kuldo cook:

"Dig a pit, build a big fire in and above the pit, put rocks on top of the fire so that as the fire burns down the rocks fall down and line the pit. When the rocks are at the bottom of the pit and the fire has burned down, put *ax* in so that it stands the way it grows, vertically. Put green hemlock boughs over this, then moss, then a thin layer of soil. Build another fire on top and keep it going all night.

"I remember cooking *ax* when I was just a kid. We just heated up a flat stone in the fire, slipped the *ax* among the white ashes, covered the plant with the hot, flat stone and after about half an hour the *ax* was cooked."

Ax has considerable food value and keeps well. As a result it warded off starvation more than once.

Freshly gathered jack pine noodles. *Opposite page:* Cutting the pine noodles. (Don't confuse the jacknife lanyard with the noodles! Both can be seen just below the cutter's hand.)

Pine Noodles

A food that must be eaten immediately upon gathering is jack pine "noodles" (<u>g</u>an hix), finely shaved strips of the sweet inner bark of the jack pine. These strips must be taken in late May or early June. An informant says:

"Very early in the morning, before daybreak, women go out to a jack pine flat. The outer bark of a young tree is cut off in handy-sized pieces and the inner juicy bark is scraped off with a bone scraper, using an up-and-down motion. Today a metal scraper is more common for this work. When the big water baskets [made of spruce root and watertight only when wet] are full, they return home."

She also told us that the noodles are eaten immediately, as the pale white shavings discolour quickly and go sour and cannot be eaten the next day. The noodles are sweet, tender and delicious, a good source of sugar. She considers that the bark has to be picked at daybreak when the sap is milky and handles easily. When the bark has been warmed by the sun, the noodles are too sticky and syrupy for her liking.

Another regular gatherer of pine noodles expressed some conflicting opinions. She says that she has cut the noodles from the trees quite late in the day with no bad results. She considers the June bark to be the best.

"You cut off the outer bark after first looking over the tree to make sure you've got a good one that hasn't too many branches and will peel well. You wipe the tree down, then begin to cut off shavings from the soft, meaty part of the tree. Our word for this dish means 'tree fat.' I use a sharp knife for this and put the shavings in a pail."

Another person added the information that she scraped her bark by "moving from left to right in nice even rows" the way she would adze a log.

Hemlock Sapwood

Most middle-aged people have tasted baked hemlock bark (xsuu'w). The following is an interesting account of its preparation:

"It's good, but you couldn't survive on it if you were starving.

"First the people make a special knife [actually a scraper] from a piece of copper. This knife (hagehlast) will be used to scrape off the inside sapwood from the bark. Sometimes if May is warm, the bark is ready. On a cold year the bark may be good right through July. They prepare food to last a week or longer and go off to a place known to be good for hemlock bark.

"When they get there, one of the wise ladies tries the taste of the sapwood. She chews it herself and scrapes off some for her partner to taste. If the sapwood tastes sour and tough, they try another tree and go on testing until they find a tree to their liking—it tastes good, sweet and tender.

"They make a camp near water and build an evergreen shelter and stay there until they have enough hemlock sapwood.

"They cut off the bark while the tree is still standing, a strip of about six feet long and three inches wide, or more. The ladies start right in scraping the inner sapwood as fast as they can. They don't let the inner bark dry.

"The ladies keep on working very hard until they have about one hundred pounds of sapwood.

"The men make a barbecue pit. They dig out the ground about four feet deep and six feet in diameter. They build a fire inside the hole until it is very dry and very hot. Then they gather stones (not too big) and line the pit. Now they build a fire on top of the rocks until the rocks are very hot.

"Now they gather clean moss and line the hot pit; they dampen this and place skunk cabbage leaves on top. On this they put the hemlock

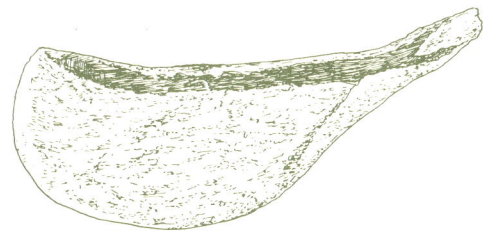

Opposite: Another pine-noodle gatherer.
Above: An early metal scraper for gathering hemlock bark

Opposite page: Crushing the hemlock bark with a wooden hammer; building the drying rack; turning the bark cakes out onto the dryer; and the cakes after they are dried. In the upper right photograph, a plastic bag is being used to keep the bark from sticking to the box. In the old days thimbleberry leaves would have been used.

sapwood, spreading it very carefully. They repeat layers of skunk cabbage and sapwood until the pit is nearly full, then they put on more skunk cabbage and then moss. When they have a good covering of moss and skunk cabbage leaves, they put on about one foot of dirt and build a fire on top which they let burn overnight. Next morning they remove the wood on top of the barbecue pit and uncover it immediately to avoid souring. If it is well cooked and tender and smells fresh, not sour, they remove the sapwood from the pit. While it is still hot they crush it....

"To crush the bark they make a four-pound hammer from a young hemlock tree. They call the younger boys and girls with strong arms to do the crushing. This is done on a crushing board [a kind of trough] made of oblong pieces of hemlock shaped just like a pig's feeder. When the sapwood is all crushed they pack it in large bent boxes and return home with a heavy load.

"When they get home they make a dryer, the same as the berry dryer. They cut off four pieces of green wood about four feet long with a fork on top. With these they make four posts which they insert in the ground like fence posts. These posts support several drying racks which are made of slats of split cedar. The overall size of the racks is about six feet long by eighteen inches wide.

"To dry the hemlock bark they prepare wooden trays one inch deep by fourteen inches by fourteen inches.

"They spread broad thimbleberry leaves in the trays to prevent the sapwood from sticking to the trays. They make syrup from the fireweed by scraping the sticky syrup from inside the wood stem. They mix the syrup with a little water and then sprinkle it on the thimbleberry leaves, then put on a layer of crushed hemlock, sprinkle it with fireweed syrup [which holds it together]. Continue this until the tray is full. Now turn the tray upside down on the wooden rack and remove the thimbleberry leaves. Build a fire underneath the dryer and keep a low fire going until each cake is dry; store the dried hemlock cakes in a wooden storage box.

"When it is to be eaten, soak it in warm water until soft. Pour oolichan grease or bear oil on the hemlock bark. Another way to serve it is to crush the cake and pour crumbs over berries.

"Today we cook it in a big kettle, being sure that the bark is not too crowded in the kettle. Line the bottom of the pot with flat rocks to prevent burning. Don't put too much water on it or it will be slushy. Dry on racks as before if you want hemlock bark to keep fresh; or put the sapwood in plastic bags and freeze; or cook it and crush it and store in the freezer; or put sapwood in jars and boil as you would for deep water bath preserving methods."

Cow parsnip, the Gitksan wild rhubarb (*Heracleum lanatum*)

Another person has this to add to the story of hemlock gathering: "To help lift the bark off you use a *hagehlast*. It's a long pole with one end shaped like a wedge or chisel. The shaped end is put under the loosened bark (beyond the bark stripper's own reach) and used to pry the bark off the tree, high up."

Fireweed

Fireweed stems just before the plant blooms furnish a substitute for sugar, being full of a sweet syrup. At that time "you cut the stems, strip off the leaves and tops, peel the silky outer covering off and serve the stem raw or roasted with oolichan grease." Fireweed stems are not dried but always eaten fresh. (More about fireweed in the section on syrups.)

Wild Rhubarb

We have two words for the plant that white people call cow parsnip. One of these words, *gatl'okwots,* applies to the plant when it is young, short, tender and edible. We translate *gatl'okwots* as wild rhubarb. Later in the summer, when the plant reaches full height, the stems are big, hard and bitter and we believe them to be poisonous. None of our group has eaten wild rhubarb after the first week in July. "After the stem begins to bulge with the second leaves, the rhubarb is bitter, tough and no good."

Wild rhubarb was split into strips before the end of June and air dried in the sun. "We used to store it away in boxes for the winter or just left it in bundles in our houses. I can remember seeing it hanging over fences and verandah rails to dry."

When eaten fresh we boiled it, or put it close to the embers of the fire for a minute or two, or ate it raw. "You have to peel off the outside skin before you cook or eat it. It's good served with fried onions and salt pork—don't cook it too long."

Wild Onions

Wild onions (*ts'anks sa gaakx*) grow plentifully on the Upper Kispiox and in other parts of the area. Our name for them literally means "Raven's underarm odour." We seldom use them now, but some know of their having been used. "Moose meat from the Upper Kispiox is flavoured with onion automatically," says one observant person with a sense of humour.

Skunk cabbage (*Lysichiton camchatcense*)

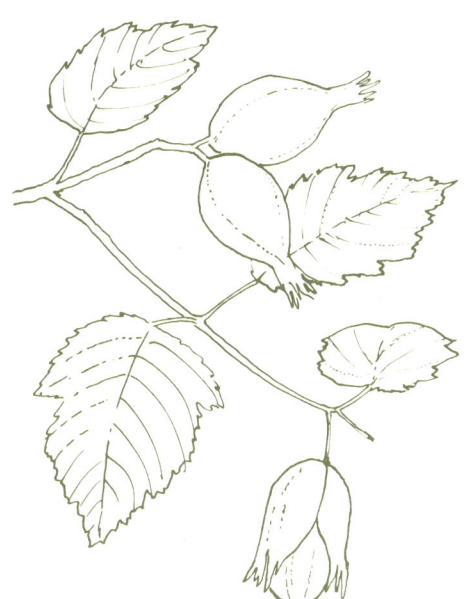

Hazelnut (*Corylus cornuta*)

Greens

Fiddlehead ferns grow in damp places all over our area. Their short shoots were boiled, baked or eaten raw with grease in the early spring, when the heads are two to six inches tall. "Our people don't eat *damtx* [fiddleheads] today."

A little rock plant, *t'ip yeest* (the common stonecrop sedum), feeds us in May or even earlier. It has small, thick leaves, juicy stems and bulbous, juicy buds. We pick the whole plant, wash it and eat it seasoned with oolichan grease (today, sugar). It grows abundantly north of Kispiox, around the falls at Moricetown, on the rocks below Kispiox, at Salmon River and on the Nass. We do not pick it for food after it flowers, but in the fall it forms berries which we pick and eat. "White people who eat it really like it."

Skunk cabbage leaves were another spring dish. The taste is strong but if the leaves are boiled once, then boiled a second time in fresh water the strong, unpleasant flavour largely disappears.

Nuts

The people we have talked with know of no nut except the hazelnut which was eaten. The tiny pine nut is plentiful but eating it is unknown today.

Gum

A small evergreen (*sk'yanadoos*) with needles like a spruce grows in the swamps, though it is fairly rare in our area. Chewy balls of gum come from these trees. "Everybody liked it, old people and kids. It turned a nice red colour when you chewed it."

This tree is plentiful north of Kuldo, and people there used lots of it and sometimes sold it—"a pocketful for fifty cents; that was a lot of money then."

Water Lily Roots

We cannot now agree on the properties of water lily roots. A drink was made by boiling them, and some believe that the mixture made a woman sterile.

Gathering spring stonecrop

Oolichan Grease from the Nass

WE HAVE MENTIONED OOLICHAN grease and some other foods which we traded for our surplus fur, skins, fat, meat or berries. The transportation of these trade foods was no easy matter. Travel conditions were cruel because the oolichans run in March or April, sometimes at the end of February. So, with great wooden boxes strapped to their backs, the old people fought their way along trails which were often buried in snow and ice. They trudged at least a hundred and thirty miles on foot to Grease Harbour on the Nass River. From there, if the river was open, they could take a canoe through treacherous waters to Fishery Bay, another forty miles away. There they got the oolichan and oolichan grease. The return trip was even tougher because the grease-filled boxes were more cumbersome and heavier than those filled with dried food.

Here is how our recorders put it:

"They would have a hard time packing the grease home. It might take them about one month to get there [Nass]. It takes longer coming back... they bring their packs in relay. They bring one ahead, then leave it and walk back and get the other pack and on it goes until they reach home. Sometimes they have three packs. They usually left early in the morning, then camped at nightfall."

Under this pack-relay system (called *gim dii yee 'asxw*), we actually walked three times to the Nass and back.

Some Gitksan hunters, whose trapping grounds lay in the Meziadin or Stewart areas, north and northeast of Fishery Bay, took their late winter's catch directly to the Nass, as they were much closer to the oolichan than to the home village. Their journey, if they followed the shortest trail, would have been every bit as hard as the trip from Kispiox or Hazelton because there is a very steep mountain range to cross.

But the lure of the grease was like the lure of gold, and every year most of our people trekked off loaded with all the surplus meat or fur they could muster to exchange for the prestigious grease, and to enjoy the reunions and trade opportunities.

This social element added lustre to the trek. The Nass oolichan fishing areas were the Mecca of the Pacific Northwest. All the peoples, for hundreds of miles in every direction, came to gather the rich grease. They came from the villages of the Tsimshian Peninsula, from Alaska, from the Queen Charlotte Islands, from the Lower Skeena, from what are now Terrace and Kitimat, and from the Upper Skeena. Annually

Rendering oolichan oil on the Nass. *Photo: British Columbia Provincial Archives*

Extracting oil with an oolichan press. *Photo: British Columbia Provincial Archives*

they gathered to fetch their year's supply of the prolific Nass oolichan run. This yearly get-together was undoubtedly a primary influence in unifying what is called the "Northwest Indian culture." The oily little fish may have played a bigger part in the lifestyle of the Indian people than is ordinarily acknowledged. All aspects of life, art styles, songs, dances, weaving techniques, carving, etc. were doubtless compared and discussed. You can picture the activity. Carvers took orders for next year's delivery; weavers traded their handiwork for grease; the basket maker took her pay in smoked oolichan; the hunter exchanged his smoked beaver for clams from the seacoast.

The coast people brought their seafoods: clams, abalone, halibut, red snapper, herring eggs, seaweed. Our people exchanged some of their furs and well-tanned skins for these coastal products. With trade in mind, we had put our dried berries into boxes which were designed to fit the racks of dried clams and oolichans that we hoped to bring home in the same boxes.

Even the animals move to the Nass when the oolichan run. "The birds are so thick they look like leaves on the trees." The oolichans swim up the river in great shoals, millions and millions of oil-rich fish. Some Nass people did so well by trading their fish catch for meat, furs and berries that they were able to exist on the gifts of the river and the trade it brought them. They could let the outsiders do the hunting and berry gathering in return for the oolichan and its golden grease; so our meat, furs and berries found a ready market.

Making Oolichan Grease

Grease-making (*sa'uyasxw*), though simple enough, is cold, round-the-clock, backbreaking work. In a very short period an enormous amount of work has to be done in order to provide a whole year's supply of grease to all the peoples of a vast area.

The fish are netted, often through holes in the ice, and dumped into bins, pits, boxes—even canoes—and left to decompose. As the fish soften, the grease oozes out, and the process is completed by boiling and skimming in the same way that fish oil is rendered (page 50).

Tastes vary, and different cooks make their grease differently. We Gitksan prefer a whiter, less ripe grease, especially when it is used with fruit. The colour and flavour of the grease depends on the length of time that the fish ripen before the grease is boiled off. The longer the fish stand, the darker the grease and the stronger the flavour.

Drying oolichans on the Nass. *Photo: British Columbia Provincial Archives*

We call the rendered grease *ha la mootxw*, which means "for curing humanity." We hear that today people are studying the nutritive properties of the oolichan's grease, expecting to learn that it is exceptionally healthful. If this is the case, it will verify our definition and confirm that oolichan grease was truly the most valuable food on our grandmother's grocery list—valuable from the standpoint of both prestige and health: caviar and cod-liver oil rolled into one.

Drying Oolichans

Though grease was our main interest, we brought back from the Nass some dried oolichans, too. We quote two interesting accounts from our files, the first called "How to dry fresh oolichan."

"Before the oolichan run they prepare the oolichan traps. This is shaped like a basketball goal (a round ring with net attached). It is a mesh of twine made out of wild linen bushes [Indian hemp] and twisted to make a net—not too big or too small. The first run of oolichan is what they dry and the rest they set aside for the oolichan grease. When they start to dry the oolichan they use a cedar rope threaded with the cedar bark string, just about one fathom in length, and hang them on a dryer. It's just like a stretcher, but they make three corners like the shape of a football goal. They use about one-half inch cedar bark rope and wrap this around the dryer, then the oolichan are dryed in the open air. When they are all dried up they take them and store them in a cool place."

The second excerpt from our files is entitled, "How to smoke fresh oolichan."

"They soak the oolichans in salt water for about twenty minutes and then drain them on wooden racks until they are all drained; then they move them into the smokehouse and hang them up. They build a fire underneath—they use alder wood—not too much fire otherwise it will spoil. They don't use fire all the time; they finish the drying in the open air."

Our wise people who furnished the information for this book do not believe that we used canoes in ancient times. The raft, yes; the canoe, no. So we could not travel far by water in search of unusual food. However, when we did get canoes—cottonwood dugouts and a few Haida canoes (which one elder calls "the cadillac of canoes")—we began to travel farther afield in search of seafoods and other edibles not available in our own territory. According to our information, most of the unusual exchange foods were sold before the traders got them home. The quick profit outweighed the gourmet in our grandfathers! It did not really matter whether the foods reached us or not because by that time the Hudson's Bay Company and other traders were on our doorsteps with all sorts of new and wonderful edibles. (See our discussion of European foods, page 98.)

Probably, even if we had had canoes, the Coast Tsimshian would have prevented us from using them, for they monopolized the food trade, and every other type of trade on the Skeena, until very recently. Some people claim that the Coast Chief Legeex established his trading rights legally in a "potlatch," but from stories of our old people, Legeex was more of a raider than a trader. (We have on file several stories of his merciless raids.) In any event, we did not travel extensively to the mouth of the Skeena for food items until the European traders opened up the route. Some of our people believe that we occasionally found our way up to the coast via the Nass. One informant points out that the Gitksan know many Haida songs, and believes that it is through journeys to the island home of those people, but there is no conclusive evidence of such travel in our files.

Beverages, Soups & Syrups

THE EXCESS JUICE from crushed raw or cooked berries is used as a beverage. The juice is drunk unstrained; in times past it was unsweetened but today, sugar is added. All varieties of juicy, edible berries are used for this drink, which we call *aksa maa'y*.

Berry juices were never fermented. We have a story about someone who drank fermented juice. "My uncle drank some rotten juice by mistake. He got dizzy and sick. He thought he was going to die. The family warned everybody not to drink it. They'd die if they did, they said."

Aksa maa'y is best when made with fresh berries; it was the highlight of summer gatherings. "We had no way of keeping it and we drank it and drank it."

"If you got to the berry patches, you had to make sure to sample each group's *aksa maa'y*.... You needed to be sure to leave room for them all or you'd hurt a lot of feelings."

Soups

Naturally, our careful ancestors saved and used all the liquid in which meat or fish was cooked. In fact, the boiled liquid was usually served right along with the meat or fish with the result that boiled meat or fish dishes were like an unthickened stew. Our recipe section gives more particulars. The whitish water that comes from boiled fish was sometimes served cold. The literal translation of our word for soup suggests that we boiled the bones to get all possible food value out of each animal.

Horsetail Reed Juice

A sweet liquid comes out of the stem of the horsetail reed. We call it by the reed's name, *maawin*. The amount of juice increases if the reed is cut and left for a few days. The horsetail provided a source of liquid for hunters who were out on the trail and away from water, perhaps above timber line. It keeps for a considerable length of time. We have a legend that tells of *maawin* as our only liquid before water came to the world. Botanists tell us that the horsetail is one of the most primitive and ancient forms of plant life. It is interesting that our legends name this primeval plant as the earliest source of water.

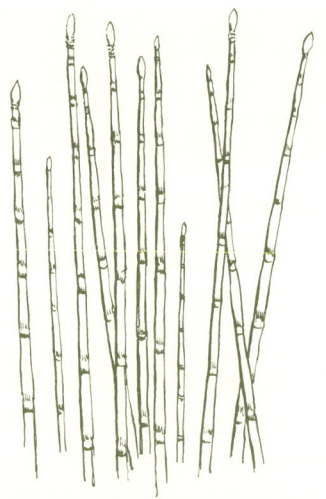

Horsetail reed (*Equisetum hyemale*)

Labrador tea bush (*Ladum groenlandicum*)

Fireweed (*Epilobium angustifolium*)

Various Teas

Hudson's Bay or Labrador tea (*sk'an dax do'oxwhl*) is made from the leaves of a shrub that grows in swampy places. The leaves, either dried or green, are placed in water and boiled. This water is poured off and replaced by fresh water which is also boiled and the resulting liquid is drunk as a beverage. It is also used as a tonic. In fact, one of our most knowledgeable elders believes that it was used only as a tonic before the white people arrived. At Kitwancool, and perhaps elsewhere, rose hips were boiled and the decoction served as a drink.

Fireweed & Other Syrups

"The fireweed's stem is filled with a syrup which can be sucked out like you suck pop through a straw." We have several accounts which state that this syrup was also used as a "glue" to keep berry rolls intact. Various sweet grasses and bark were also used as syrups, though none of our teachers has actually sampled anything but fireweed and pine-bark syrup. Some claim to have used fireweed syrup to sweeten soapberry froth.

Informants are convinced that pine sap was taken in spring the way maple sap is taken in other areas, but no one has actually seen this done except by non-Indians.

Other Edible Plants

SOME BERRIES AND PLANTS which we now know to be edible were not used by our forefathers. One puzzling omission is the entire mushroom family. It is puzzling because no poisonous mushrooms grow here, and all of the best varieties are plentiful. Some local varieties might make us sick and some could produce hallucinations, but none could kill us.

We have records of a substance called *win do'o* which seemingly produced sleep and even made people appear to be dead. As yet, we have been unable to learn the ingredients of *win do'o*. We are told only that it came in "a kind of cake, like chewing tobacco." It could be that the hallucination-producing mushroom was one component and that all mushrooms were therefore suspect, or made suspect by the knowledgeable few who wished to keep secret the recipe for this substance. We are told by some that mushrooms were not eaten because lizards and frogs crawled on them.

The edibility of rose hips has already been discussed (page 74).

Nettles (*statxs*) and plantain (*tkwa'ltxw*), if they were ever food items, have been forgotten as such. We have no record of our neighbours having used them either, but we have names for both. We have noticed that plants which have no specific uses often have no name. Nettles, of course, made twine, but plantain, unless it was used as a medicine, had no other use than as a food.

Plantain (*Plantago major*)

Foods of Our Ancestors

The botanists list many edible plants native to our area but which are not in our group's food records. We must have used some of them. In search of further information so that we could give a complete list of our grandparents' menu possibilities, we have read all the available literature. In *Notes on the Western Dénés,* by Rev. A.-G. Morice, we found abundant information concerning the eating habits of our next-door neighbours, the Carriers. Since we traded extensively with them, it is safe to say that edible plants which grow in our area as well as theirs were probably used by our ancestors, too. Today, most of our neighbours are unaware that the plants were ever eaten by them or anyone else.

This is what Father Morice has added to our information:

"The Western Dénés [Carriers] find in their immediate vicinity several indigenous plants to diversify their daily menu of fish or meat. Chief

Red lily (*Lilium columbianum*)

among these may be quoted the red lily (*Lilium columbianum*) the bulb of which is used as an article of food by most British Columbians... or even Asiatic tribes. It is cooked by boiling pretty much as is done with potatoes. The natives harvest it almost as soon as it has sprouted out, a short time after the disappearance of snow....

"Another plant of a different botanical family whose root is likewise much appreciated as an article of food is the sweet flag (*Acorus calamus*). This root is eaten without any other preparation than cleaning and washing in cold water.

"The wild onion is also eaten, root and leaves, either raw or slightly roasted in the ashes.... so is the root of the dog tooth violet.

"In the cow parsnip (*Heraculeum lanatum*) it is the inner part of the growing stalk that is preferred. It is often used while fresh and unprepared save by the stripping of its fibrous envelope. But if fire is at hand a Carrier will generally treat it to a slight roasting through the flames previously to peeling off the stalk.

"The marrow of the willow herb (*Epilobium angustifolium*) [Fireweed] is also much esteemed.... it is eaten before the plant reaches maturity.

"Nor do the Carrier disdain the leaves of the oregon grape (*Berberis* [or *Mahonia*] *aquafolium*) which are simmered in a little water until no liquid remains.

"Another article of food, cheap because very common but prized by the aborigines is the hair-like lichen (*Alectoria jubata*), which grows hanging from the trees."

Food After the Europeans Came

TODAY, OF COURSE, we eat all the foods that other Canadians eat, as well as many of our own traditional foods. In the old days we had no sugar or salt, and some think that was why we were so healthy. Now we use sugar and salt, even with many of our traditional foods, and are very fond of sweet carbonated drinks. We still "go easy" on the salt.

At first, we found the white man's food strange and sometimes wonderful. A story is told that a man came to Kitsegas selling, out of a can, handfuls of stuff that could be made into a drink. Some of our people decided that whenever someone old drank this "stuff" — which was coffee — he would become almost young again. For a while coffee was a great seller!

Another story is told that the first time bread was seen in one village the people didn't know what it was or what to do with it, so they put it on the berry drying racks. When the bread was very dry, they broke it into pieces and gave it as a plaything to the children, who threw it at one another. Children today like bread and eat a great deal of it, but many of the older people still do not eat much bread. A man of seventy told us that he ate bread only rarely, and then only to be polite.

The cow's advent caused consternation. "A herd of cattle were driven through our country in the early days, when my mother was a teenager," one informant reported, referring to the disastrous Yukon cattle drive. At Kuldo, these strange new creatures terrified those who saw them. We did not readily accept the milk these cows gave. "Don't give it to your children," a grandmother told one of our reporters. "It will make them wild like animals."

"One day grandfather took us out fishing at Spencers. A white man there invited us in to eat. His name was Spencer so they called the place after him.... He cooked rice. There was Granny and Gramps, Grace and I. The man put some cooked rice in a dish and put fresh milk in it for each of us and I couldn't eat it. I wanted to throw up instead; my stomach would turn over and over. So Louise told me to push it aside. She said, 'The white man might see you throw up.' So I pushed my dish away from me. After they all finished eating then we left and Grandfather bawled me out. He said, 'You dog. You real dog. The white man was doing us an honour by giving you milk and rice and here you wouldn't eat it. He was treating you like a real person.' I never did eat it.

He put sugar with it but I didn't like the fresh milk he put in with it. Later on it seemed really funny to me. I still laugh about it."

We were suspicious of the new foods, but not of the containers, which could not poison anyone, and immediately found uses for the cans, bottles and boxes in which the foods were packaged.

Bread & Bannock

Once bread was accepted, most people quickly learned to make unleavened biscuit dough, the quick bread we call bannock. They also learned to bake bread leavened with yeast and baking powder, sometimes cooking it in the Indian-style oven. We have a description from as late as 1910 of baking in an earth oven using tins and a tin cover (another bread pan turned upside down) to protect the dough from the leaf and earth covering and allow room for the bread to rise.

Bread-on-a-stick is an interesting combination of old and new that enables us to cook bread over a campfire. Bread dough or baking powder biscuit dough can be wound around one end of a stake and tied on with string wrapped around it like a bandage. The other end of the stake is driven into the earth at such an angle that it holds the dough over the fire while it bakes. The stake is frequently turned so that all sides of the bread bake evenly. When the dough is cooked, you pull out the string and eat a nice hot biscuit.

Other favourites among white man's foods are crackers and pilot bread, which keep well and are easy to serve. A delicious adaption of new food to our traditional way of cooking occurs when we fry pilot biscuits in oolichan grease.

Potatoes

Missionaries and traders introduced potatoes, "which just about everyone grows today." We believe that our name for potato—*gusiit*—came from the missionaries telling our people that it was "good seed." We have come to enjoy this vegetable, especially with fish, and the crop requires little attention so that it can be tended by the people who go to the canneries in the summer.

Because of their annual expedition to the canneries, most people have little time to spend on gardening and therefore grow only easily tended crops. Most of those who stay home have good-sized, well-tended vegetable gardens in which root crops predominate.

New Foods, New Words

Contact with English-speaking people brought new words to our food vocabulary as well as new foods to our tables. We handled these innovations in a variety of ways. Sometimes we used a descriptive phrase from our own language, as in the case of our word for an enamel cup, *hlabal weex,* which means "the price of one lynx." Sometimes we changed the English word a little, as in the case of *tsigins* for chickens, *dee* for tea, *abbles* for apples. Sometimes we made up a word which described some characteristic of the new things, as we do when we call the cow *mismuus.*

3

Some Hints for Cooks

In our food discussions, we have slipped in the occasional recipe or cooking hint. People have asked us to also include cooking instructions for some of our less common dishes. We have hesitated because our senior cooks tend to cook by their visual memory of what they have seen their elders do and by their own cooking sense gained through long experience. They measure by "potfuls," "handfuls," and "little bits," rather than by level teaspoons, cups, pounds or ounces, and they improvise a great deal.

With those facts on record, we are going to give you some unedited cooking instructions from our elders. We would like you to feel that you are sitting around a campfire, or in someone's kitchen, swapping cooking know-how with friends.

If you have done a fair amount of cooking you will have no trouble following the instructions, and they may provide you with some new dining adventures.

Soups

Fishbone Soup

"When you're canning fish you save out everything you don't can, like the fins and the head and the backbone and the tail, and you boil this all up, slow, gentle, just enough. You season it any way you like. Curry's good, and celery salt and onions. It's good lots of ways. You eat the meaty parts—every bit of that fish head is delicious. Maybe it's more of a mulligan than a soup by the time you fix it up—and boiled rice is just right with it—flaky boiled rice. Make sure you eat every bit of meat off that backbone and head. They're the best of the fish."

Fish Chowder (Hagul Jam)

"You take real fresh salmon and cut it up into fairly small pieces. Never use fish that's been dead for a while. Put a pot of salted water on to boil, add some cut-up onions and sometimes potatoes, peeled and cut into bit-sized chunks. Put the fish in last. Be sure the fish is really fresh. Add curry powder if you like. It is good with curry powder in it. Don't boil the fish too long, not more than twenty minutes at the most. Serve in nice big, deep bowls." Each person always had more than one bowl.

Another informant adds this information:

"Fish eggs and the inside parts of fish are good in *hagul jam,* too. The backbone makes the broth richer. You can slowly boil the backbones and insides in the water for quite a while, then add the vegetables and the fish."

Village Soup (Sibim G̲al Ts'ap)

This is the soup that we make for feasts in the villages. Each cook has her own special way of doing it. Here's one way to make a "nice big pot for twenty people."

"Brown three pounds or more of moose, caribou or goat meat cut into small chunks, the right size to eat in one mouthful.

"Cover with water to within two inches of the top of a big (two-gallon) pot and simmer until meat is almost tender, then add an assortment of cut-up vegetables that might include carrots, onions, turnips, celery and peas. Put in lots of potatoes, cubed. Cook until the vegetables are done. Macaroni may be used, too, but it is inclined to stick if the soup has to be kept hot on a stove for a long time—and as that is often the case at our feasts, most of us leave out the macaroni.

"Salt and pepper the soup to taste and have a tin of curry powder handy for those who want to add that spice."

Breads

Pan Bread

"Mix a fairly stiff dough of flour and water. Do not include yeast or baking powder but use some grease. Put the mixture into heavy, greased iron frying pans. Cook the dough on one side, turn it over and cook it on the other side. Eat it while it's hot." This dish, called x̲sax̲ t'iisa, requires no punching or kneading.

Bannock & Bannock-Style Bread

"Mix some grease, about one-half cup, no more than that, into flour (about two cups, I guess); add salt and four teaspoons of regular baking powder (two teaspoons of quick-rising baking powder). Add water to make a thick dough. Knead this well, really well. Put the kneaded dough into heavy, greased iron frying pans. Be sure to grease the sides as well as the bottom of the pan. Fill the pans halfway up the sides. Move the pan around on the campfire so that the dough cooks evenly. When the bannock will slip in the pan, turn it over and cook the other side—like a pan-cake. Some people put sugar and milk in. The old people made this into loaves, too, and cooked it in ovens. To make the dough real close and firm like they made it you have to knead hard, a lot; otherwise it's like baking powder biscuits. Bannock bread should be very close textured. Keep your bannocks hot, beside the fire, until you are ready to eat them."

Fried Bread

"You can make this with yeast dough or baking powder biscuit dough. It's not an ancient food. It's best with yeast dough. After your dough has risen once, you put it out in little flat cakes, something like a small pancake, and let these little cakes rise. When they are about double in size, drop them into deep fat, medium hot to hot. Some people pull and stretch this dough; others just pop it into the fat. They musn't be cooked too long; it makes them tough. Some cooks just drip the dough, after it's risen once, into the fat. This makes a heavier type of fried bread. Most of us prefer it lighter."

Fish

Baked Fish Heads (Uuda T'im Ges)

"Place washed fish heads in a roasting pan that's been greased. Cook the heads about sixty minutes in a medium oven, until the skin is nice and crisp and the meat just done. The cheek meat's good; everything's good. Salt and pepper it well. Serve it with whatever you like. Fish heads are rich so salad's good with them, but most people use potatoes. Spring salmon's generally used, but other salmon are good too. Never throw any of them away."

Buts'

This is an L-shaped piece in the stomach of a fish. Another word for it is the same as our word for elbow adze—*t'axwinst*: the adze and the fish's bodily organ are shaped the same.

One cook has these comments about *buts'*:

"Use them fresh only, never smoked. Flour them well. Fry them in good hot grease until brown. Do not overcook. Serve right away, with potatoes or whatever you have. Dogs don't like them."

Fish Hearts (Gal K'oop)

"When you are smoking or canning fish be sure to save out all the fish hearts. They make a good dish by themselves. They can be cooked all sorts of ways. Maybe baking them in the oven is best. Just put them with grease in a roasting pan, salt them and bake them. Fried in a heavy pan, in grease, on top of the stove with onions is nice too. One of the best parts of the fish is the heart. If you don't cook them separately,'be sure to put them in your *hagul jam* [fish soup]."

Boiled Fish Backbone

"I usually smoke the backbones a while, then boil up a dozen or so at a time. They cook quickly. Eating that meat off the backbone is like eating good pork spareribs. Meat close to bones is the best meat in fish or animals." For this dish, called *jam k'yo'o*, we use spring salmon only.

Salted Fish

"Salted fish, *mo'onim hon,* and boiled potatoes make a good meal. Soak the fish overnight. Boil in fresh water. Boil potatoes separately. Serve with grease—oolichan—if you have any."

Toasted Half-dried Fish ('Nii Bahla'am Ts'al)

"To toast half-dried fish, place it beside or over a fire by any of the toasting or barbecuing methods. Cook the meat side first, a little bit, then turn and toast the skin side until crisp."

Boiled Fully Dried Salmon (Jamksxw)

"Take some dried fish and soak it overnight. Boil it plain or with onions in the water. Serve with boiled potatoes."

Salted Fish Belly (Mo'onim Ts'ok̲xw)

"Take the salted fish and soak it overnight in cold water. Change the water and bring to the boil. Boil just a few minutes. Serve with plain boiled potatoes. The *ts'ok̲xw* is very rich and needs no extra dressing." (In past times when people really needed fat foods and when fat foods were our "treats," this part of the fish was esteemed above all others.)

Fried Seaweed (P'ah'loosxw)

"The loose seaweed, not the dried cakes, is fried for a few seconds in boiling grease in a pan. Put the grease in the pan, heat it, put in the seaweed and turn it over after a few seconds. Cook it for half a minute on the other side. Take it out of the pan immediately and serve."

Fish Eggs

Herring Eggs (Xs'wink̲x)

"However you cook them, they're good. I usually put a pot of water on the stove and when it boils pop in the eggs. They musn't boil too long or they get tough. You can serve them with potatoes or boiled seaweed and oolichan grease or rice."

Boiled Fish Eggs & Seaweed

This dish — *luu 'lanim hlok̲asxw* — is usually made with spring salmon eggs, but all types of salmon eggs are used on occasion. These eggs are cooked, when fresh, by boiling a short time in salted water. "Do not overcook them; it toughens them. Just use enough water to cover the eggs. When the eggs are done, stir in the seaweed to the thickness you prefer. We serve it so that it's like very soft and fluffy whipped potatoes. Serve it hot, as soon as cooked."

Here is another description: "I usually boil the eggs in just a little water. I only boil them a minute. I take off that kind of scum that forms. I add seaweed to the hot water and eggs until the mixture is like a thick sauce and the seaweed just soft. Most people add oolichan grease to this, but I don't."

Fried Herring Eggs

"Down at Namuu Cannery, lots and lots of herring eggs used to be piled up on the seaweeds. We'd take big cakes of them, fry them in a frying pan, first on one side, then turn them over like a pancake and fry the other side. We all used to go for this."

Fish Eggs & Oolichan Grease

"If the eggs are dried, soak them until soft and puffed out and round. If the eggs are salted, wash them until they suit your taste and are just salty enough. Put eggs in cooking pot. Add water until you can just see it. Heat water just to boiling point; don't boil. Add oolichan grease. Stir well and serve hot. Especially enjoyable if served with seaweed and rice."

Toasted Seeweed (Sa Xulgwa)

"Warm the seaweed for a few minutes over a fire—not very long. Crumble it up and serve it on top of fish soup or herring eggs or just nibble on it. Anyone who enjoys seafood will enjoy seaweed."

Meat

Boiled Moose Nose

"My husband cooks it. When we had a cook stove that burned wood, he used to put the moose nose right in the stove in the fire. Now he goes outside and builds a fire, a hot one. He leaves the nose in the fire until all the hair's off, in the nostrils and all. (It is pure white when it's ready to come off.) Then he scrapes all that outside hard stuff off and boils the meat. He fixes it up with spices and onions in the water, just whatever he thinks of. It can't be cooked too long. It is more tender if it hangs awhile."

Another says, "This is the best part of the moose. You can put it in the smokehouse for a day or two before cooking it if you like the smoked flavour. It can be boiled or it can be roasted in the oven."

Smoked & Roasted Porcupine

"Cut it first. Burn quills off in the fire. It needs lots of heat. The quills form a whitish crust which you can peel off. Smoke it whole, that is, in one flat piece and all bones removed. It tastes best cooked over an open fire. Leave it in the smokehouse for a day or two to give it a good flavour and tenderize the meat a little. Cook it by any of the roasting methods."

Roast Rabbit Ears

"My dad used to toast rabbit ears until they were crispy and curly. We kids used to sit around waiting for them to get done just right. He started off by singeing off all the fur; then he held the ears strung on a long stake over the coals, not the flames. They musn't get in the flames."

Fried Rabbit Innards (Ts'eewa G̲ax̲)

"Mother took hours cleaning and fixing the inside parts of a rabbit. Dad would get lots of them some years. Just lots. No one would go to the trouble now to fix up and clean these insides, but Mother did it and she fixed them by putting flour on them and frying them in nice clean grease. The best innards of all is beaver's."
Another informant describes this food as a quick lunch.
"I remember, my uncle, when he got some rabbit, would tie the small intestines around a roasting stick and cook them over the fire. You suck out the hot inside part. In the winter you got vitamins this way, that you couldn't get yourself, because the rabbits turned it into food for you."

Barbecued Beaver Tail

"The main thing to remember about beaver tail is not to overcook it—it goes to mush. My Dad used to take the tail and scorch it real good over the campfire—the hide peels right off then. After that you barbecue it just long enough. The outside would be nice and crisp and you can get it crisp if you put it where the fire's real hot, at the last."

Half-smoked Bear Intestines

"Cut into two-foot lengths. Smoke for at least two days, using rotted white poplar for your wood. Boil for two or more hours. Don't boil hard, but keep it simmering for a good long time."

Boiled Moose Intestines

"This is very rich. Take a long time to clean it and then clean it some more. Cut it into small pieces and boil it. (Some people put it in the smokehouse for a while.)"

Another person said: "When they're cooked they don't need anything with them. You can only eat a little because it's so rich, so much fat with it, that inside fat. All we serve is potatoes."

Roast Marrow (K'itsa'i)

"When they've killed and skinned a moose they cut the meat off the leg and put the bone in a really hot fire—really hot. When the bone is thoroughly heated, they break it in two and eat the marrow."

Mountain Goat Tripe

"This is so good that sometimes a hunter hides it from the rest and saves it for himself. Wash it and boil it. It cooks fairly quickly."

Wild Meat

"Mountain goat, moose, caribou and even deer can be dry and flavourless. You can overcome this.

"Get a good-sized piece of heavy tinfoil, big enough to wrap your roast in. Get a package of onion soup mix, any good brand. Wash your roast. While the roast's still wet, put a package of onion soup mix on top of the roast. Spread it all over the top of the roast. Put beef suet on top of this. Fold your tinfoil up around the roast so that all the juices are sealed in. Put your roast in a covered roasting pan in a moderate oven and cook it twenty-five minutes to the pound. When it's done, take off the foil, let the juice spill into the roasting pan. Make a nice onion gravy out of the pan juices and pour it over mashed potatoes."

Desserts

Yal Is

"Clean one-half cup of freshly picked green or ripe [soap]berries. Put in large basin and crush or squeeze the berries. Remove all seeds. [Today we usually use a wire sieve for this and force the crushed pulp through the sieve into the bowl.] Add water to the seeded berry pulp—about one-quarter cup. Whip rapidly with the hand until the mixture's creamy. [An egg beater is faster but less 'authentic.'] Add half a cup or more of sugar, slowly, while beating. Continue beating until the mixture resembles stiffly beaten egg whites, except that it's pinkish.

"You may serve *yal is* by piling it into tulip cups or any fancy dessert glasses you may have." (On page 62 you have seen our way of eating this dessert.)

"*Yal is* will not hold its shape for long. It stays fluffy longer if you put the bowl in a cold place. Best way is to keep beating it until you serve it.

"A small quantity of crushed berries makes a large bowl of *is*. Be sure your bowl is big enough and that it's absolutely free of grease.

"*Yal is* is a good dessert after a heavy meal."

Sun-dried Soapberries

"I dry mine on sheets of paper or canvas. I spread out the berries on the sheets and dry them in the sun until they are really dry. I shake them around on the sheet. They taste just like fresh berries so long as they are kept in an airtight container."

Dayks

"Place about a gallon of nice, powdery snow in a large basin. Pour in, gradually, about one cup of oolichan grease and beat rapidly by hand until a foamy, creamy consistency. Take a cupful of snow and pour a half cup of water over the snow. Let the water go through the snow, drain, pour it into the blended mixture. Add berries and serve. A varying quantity of berries is used, depending on taste. The best berries for this are huckleberries, high and low bush cranberries and blueberries. *Dayks* looks something like berries mixed with a white yogurt."

4

Food In Our Lives

Etiquette

OF COURSE, BOOKS on etiquette did not exist in ancient days, but unwritten rules as rigid as any written ones were strictly observed in every aspect of living, including the serving and eating of food.

Today, we go along with the Canadian version of "manners" in most cases and as a result, some rules of past times seem peculiar to our young people. However, those ancient rules were, in their time, just as sensible as some dictates of the modern code, and adherence to the rules of the time was obligatory for the nobility.

A child learned that it was shameful to spill food at any time, but food spilled at a feast damaged the reputation of the entire family. The family, or the person guilty of the misdemeanour, called a "shame" feast (*tl'okxw* feast) almost immediately in order to wipe out the blot on the family name.

A well-brought-up person did not speak unnecessarily while eating, nor did he refuse proffered food. If there was more than he could possibly eat he simply packed the food in a container and carried it home without any noisy thank yous. Nor did he make verbal comments about the food he was eating. A satisfied smack of the lips and a loud and convincing burp told volumes. At the close of a formal feast, all visiting chiefs gave eloquent addresses in which they praised the hosts and expressed in glowing terms appreciation of the food they had been served.

Men were served before women and children unless the woman was a chief with a very important name — an unusual situation in times past. If there were guests the women of the host household did not sit down to eat but tended to the needs of the visitors. At feasts none of the hosts is seated; both men and women administer to the guests' welfare. (This was not true at Kitwancool, the Gitksan village closest to the Nass River, which had its own rules.)

Not too long ago, the person who served a chief never looked the chief in the eye but kept his or her eyes respectfully downcast. Very special care had to be taken when serving a *halayt* (medicine man or woman). No one could pass in front of a *halayt* who was eating, nor could anyone make a noise; otherwise the *halayt* might swallow the offender's life spirit along with the meal.

In the past it was good manners to serve guests an almost embarrassing amount of food. Now, as then, it is obligatory at feasts to provide more food than the guests can eat. All guests, therefore, bring containers

Carved wooden food dish from 'Ksan

in which to carry home the superabundance, or *so'o*, from a feast. Formerly, guests also brought their own tableware; today, some invitations remind guests to bring "cup, bowl and spoon."

In ancient times only chiefs attended feasts, and the hosts saw to it that each chief had sufficient *so'o* to feed all the members of his family who had remained at home.

We have among our recorded songs some which are to be sung when food is served. Opinions vary as to the precise usage of these songs, but certainly some were a welcome and some were an invitation to the guests to begin to eat. Among our informants, a few consider the songs to be of the nature of a grace before beginning the meal.

There are also records telling of a period of unified silence, a mode of offering thanks to the Great Nature for having supplied the food. Such customs are not described in any of our recorded legends, but elders insist that they existed.

How Food Shaped the Way of the Gitksan

CULTURES, LIKE ARMIES, march on their stomachs. If there is insufficient food and empty stomachs, the culture marches nowwhere; with plenty of food and full stomachs, the culture marches ahead.

In normal years we had lots of food and our culture marched ahead. In fact, because of a plentiful food supply throughout the Pacific Northwest, the ancient Indian culture marched farther ahead than that of any nonagricultural people of any place at any time.

We cannot now know whether or not it was because of the abundance of food that feasts, the so-called potlatches, came to be the focal point of our economic, civil and social life. We *do* know that, for one reason or another, all our activities centred around feasts; no business of any consequence was done except at a feast. "We successfully combined business with pleasure: the pleasure of good food and good entertainment. We had feasts for marriage and feasts to get a divorce, feasts to make war and feasts to make peace, feasts to assess damage and feasts to pay debts, feasts for birth and feasts for death, feasts to acquire land and feasts to give it away, feasts for you-name-it." Without a good supply of food this feasting could not have taken place.

Partly because of the availability of a good supply of food, there is a striking difference between the quantity of food served at our feasts and the quantity served at an average banquet, and an equally striking difference in the way we deal with the food after we serve it. We provide food not only to feed our guests but also as an enhancement, something to make more memorable the legal transactions for which the feast is called. Food is also part of a guest's "gift-payment" for doubling as a guest-witness to the business which is being conducted at the feast. Consequently, guests at a feast expect the host family to provide a generous amount of take-home food. This superabundance of food is called *so'o*. At a big feast, *so'o* piles up high beside every important guest. When that guest leaves he usually has more gifts and payments than one man can carry, much of which is *so'o*. In former times, several lower-ranking people hauled home a great chief's gifts and *so'o* for him; today, he carries it himself. In the past there was probably more to carry because only the chiefs attended the feasts and the *so'o* was taken back by the leaders to their tribesmen so that all could share the magnanimity and generosity of the host chief and his family.

One ancient feast—<u>x</u>so'omsxw (consuming *so'o*)—seems at first glance to have been given solely to distribute *so'o*. Closer examination of the facts shows what really happened: When a chief's high-ranking messengers (*thets*) delivered invitations to a great feast (*yukxw*) they were given huge quantities of *so'o* by the chiefs receiving the invitations. When the invitation-bearers returned home, they in turn gave a feast and divided the *so'o* among the guests. These recipients were expected to billet the chiefs who sent the *so'o* when they came as guests to the great feast. In today's business language the *so'o* was actually an advance payment for future hospitality, a deposit for future room and board.

Gyaba' (literally, "to ladle") is a payment in food seldom witnessed now. *Gyaba'* was frequently paid to a chief who had been "given a bad time" publicly in a teasing song as part of the entertainment at a feast, usually at the *bagwansxw,* or welcome feast. Having been the target of the fun-loving group's satirical songs, the chief was then *very* quickly presented with an impressive gift of food. *Gyaba'* is also the term applied to lavish food gifts given to the highest chiefs at feasts and usually took the form of an immense ladleful of oolichan grease or crushed berries.

Another extra special gift for the highest chiefs is called *batsa*, which means to lift up something. The impressive gift, often a whole bent cedar box of rare food, is lifted up high in the air, while the name of the illustrious recipient is called out twice, loudly.

Guests came to these feasts prepared: their assistants (nephews) brought empty spruce root baskets, birch baskets, or bent boxes. In more recent times, clean flour sacks and empty pillow cases were brought along for the dry foods and jars for the juicy ones. Today, brown paper bags and good-sized cardboard cartons are used for dry foods and plastic containers for moist ones.

Women made their obligatory contributions to feasts largely in the form of food. They provided many, many rolls of dried berries, boxes of *hlayax* (berries or crab apples mixed with grease), bundles of dried fish. Every chief expected to take home at least one giant box of dried fruit, and the women of the host's family provided this as their share of the cost of the feast. Today, the apples and oranges given away at feasts are named after their predecessors, the old bent wood boxes (*xgal'inkx*) which formerly contained berry rolls, crab apples and other delicacies.

Food as Intermediary with the Powers Beyond

We have some information, although it is inconclusive, about our use of food as an intermediary between us and the Powers Beyond the Human who could influence our lives. Our legendary helper, Mouse

Woman, may ask us to throw fat in the fire, but she invariably retrieves it unharmed—the food does not go up in smoke. Does throwing this fat in the fire constitute a real sacrifice? The human whom Mouse Woman assisted purchased the little lady's help by giving away food, and to some extent it was a sacrifice. But it was a very practical one and guaranteed to succeed because everyone knew that if you saw the little mouse and did as she commanded, no harm would come to you. Thus it was not a true sacrifice but more like a payment for services to be rendered.

In *Tsimshian Mythology* the anthropologist Franz Boas cites many Coast Tsimshian legends in which food is burned in a sacrificial manner. Since we are close cultural relatives of the Coast people we must pay attention to Boas, for we have many almost identical legends. One in particular fits our purpose here: the tale of the Snail and the Princess. As Boas tells it, five of the Princess' six brothers unsuccessfully attempt to rescue her. Their assistants burn quantities of food while their masters search. The sixth brother, when his turn comes, instructs his assistants to burn food and food and more food. He succeeds. We Gitksan have essentially the same story, except that there is no burning of food, which would have been considered wasteful.

We are told that once, when a terrible fog covered a mountain top, the trapped hunters built a fire and "burned a small, little fish," and the fog lifted. This fish is definitely a burnt offering, but a "small, little" burnt offering—no squandering of food. The token offering satisfied the Powers Beyond.

Our legends seem to indicate that wood smoke and the warm fire itself constituted our means of winning support from Beyond, as witness this prayer: "Grandfather, Grandfather! Who will keep your fires burning if you let us die?" Since we did not have the same superabundance of food as the Coast people had, we tended to save our food for our food cellars and food mats, and showed respect for the Powers by keeping a wood fire burning rather than burning food on that fire.

The abnormal occurred when food was burned by those frantically trying to "cure" a man possessed by the dreaded Man Eaters', or Dog Eaters', Power. (The Man Eaters and Dog Eaters were two of four so-called Secret Societies.) More than one competent elderly historian has recorded stories about the Man Eaters and Dog Eaters in which food is burned to influence the Power.

This raises an interesting question, because the Man Eaters and Dog Eaters evolved at the same time that the traders first came to our area. Did the new-found wealth of the fur trade reduce the value of food so that our people began to waste it? Or did the Man Eater and Dog Eater

Power have such influence that we were willing to destroy food to appease it?

Food for the Dead

We know we burned food on the cremation pyres because our present term for the flowers that we give at funerals means "to make a pack lunch for someone other than yourself to take on a journey" (*ts'ilimdinhl*) and is derived from the custom of putting food into the hands of the corpse on the pyre. Other food was probably also burned with the corpse. Later, food was put in the gravehouses and has been seen there by many of our informants. The food was left to feed the deceased's afterlife self, the *hayxw,* in the Beyond.

Similarly, when a burning log hissed, the dead signalled their presence, and usually their need of food. Someone immediately responded by tossing a little bit of food into the fire—"not a lot, but some."

Stories have circulated concerning the burial of food at the bases of totem poles. While restoring poles in our villages, the bases of more than twenty poles were excavated. Only one food package was found, so it cannot have been a very common practice. We cannot tie in this belief to the beliefs that survive in the memories of those living today.

Food as a Symbol

Food plays the leading role in a preparation-for-war ceremony where, as the symbol of blood, crushed red berries incited warriors to action:

"The ladies squeezed berries in a big wooden box; then Owl jumped up and poked his spear [through] it and cracked the box so that the berries poured out of it (looking like blood). The other warriors with him then did the same until there was nothing left [of the box] and the berries were all over the ground."

The chief who was organizing the war party gave a blanket to each man who took part in the destruction of the box. Acceptance of the blanket was a guarantee of active support. In this instance we were extravagant with food for a practical reason.

Oolichan grease assumed the role of blood in war-making ceremonies among our cousins at the mouth of the Skeena, according to Boas. One local expert believes that we, too, used it in a similar manner, drinking huge ladlefuls to indicate symbolically that we would take the life blood of our foes.

Purposeless or extravagant destruction of food at feasts has not been mentioned by any of our own historians. However, grease was thrown on fires during festivities, not as a wasteful or scornful gesture but for practical purposes. Maybe a burst of bright light was essential to the dramatization of the Na*x* No*k*. Or maybe a *halayt* (medicine man) needed more heat or a brighter light to effect a cure. Or perhaps intense, bright light should enhance the robing of a new chief. But whatever the practical need, one thing was certain: we did not waste what the Great Nature had provided. We might reincarnate the eaten creature by carefully burning every bone, but we did not squander any edible part in the flames.

Certain ceremonies and entertainments, or parts of them, related to a specific kind of food. By far the most important of these specialized feasts was the annual celebration of the arrival of the first spring salmon. We have found no one who has actually celebrated this event, but several people have given us information which their elders passed on to them. Accounts differ. Here are the facts we have gleaned:

The arrival of the first salmon each spring triggered a special ceremony, a ceremony of gratitude.

This ceremony was a solemn one.

The moment the first salmon appeared in the net or fish trap—perhaps a single fish, perhaps a school of a dozen or so early fish—the fish were carried ceremoniously to the village, some say on a cedar mat. Their exact destination in the village is debated—perhaps the smokehouse, perhaps the house of the owner of the trap, perhaps the house of the head chief.

Each fish was laid out on a separate, clean, woven cedar mat.

Eagle down was sprinkled on the fish. (There is debate as to who spread it; "the highest chief" is the most common answer.)

Another clean mat was placed on top. (This information is controversial.)

No one in the village spoke during the entire night. (This is agreed among all informants and is emphasized.)

The next morning there was an expression of thanks. (Its form is unclear.)

The fish were then either roasted whole or boiled whole (opinions differ and probably both are correct), then cut into portions so that every man, child and eligible woman received a piece. *Xhlaxws,* the traditional name for this portion which each person received, refers to the skewers inserted in the fish to stabilize it during the cooking process.

Some say the head chief distributed the fish.

No accompanying song or dance is remembered, but most informants are sure that such songs or dances existed.

Several historians stress the idea that "our ancestors gave thanks to a Force Bigger than Themselves for having once again sent the life-preserving fish."

Food & Fun

During the month-long "potlatch" there was an entertainment which has been described to us in contradictory statements and fragmentary details. None of our informants actually took part. Here are a few recollections:

"People dressed funny."

"They marched through the village and made lots of noise—*lots* of noise."

"They marched into houses and yelled for the hardest things to make or get. You got that food or they [the householders] were in deep trouble."

"Maybe it was their hallowe'en."

Yal is, or frothberry whip, was featured in some welcome feasts as a dare to the highest chiefs.

"Guests heard the distant sound of women singing about *yal is*. The sound comes closer and closer until there is a loud knocking on the door and a bunch of ladies dance in with great big bowls of *yal is* which they hold on one arm while they whip it [*yal is*] up with the other hand. They are twirling themselves round and round and swaying back and forth as they sing and whip the *yal is*. Then each dancer picks out a big chief and plops down in front of him and he has to eat the whole bowl, else he's in trouble." The Chief's nephews were allowed to help him.

We also have several stories concerning the use of enormous quantities of grease, rum, berry juice and other edibles as dares. Although none is definitely confirmed by a second informant, everyone believes that these contests were held, sometimes as a challenge to an enemy but more often in the spirit of fun that prevailed at the welcome feasts.

Other feast tales record the existence of tribal specialties as party foods.

"This was a specialty of the Fireweed [phratry] in that village. There were big copper boilers full of mashed potatoes, and they served this with sugar. They also served baking powder dough and bread dough fried in deep oolichan grease heated in a big black pot. They did this in the fall of the year. They always had lots and lots and everyone took home lots and lots."

"The Wolves [members of the Wolf phratry], when the first snow came, had this feast—not a serious feast, just a fun entertainment, but they did it every year. They'd mix oolichan grease with snow. They'd soak dried berries, add sugar and pour it on top of the snow and oolichans—an Indian sundae! In those days there was no tonsilitis because they ate big chunks of xay mooxws, as we call it."

Another informant adds more to this description of the Wolf Feast:

"The Wolves acted like wolf cubs playing in the snow. They rolled around the floor, pretended to scoop up snow with their noses like wolf cubs do, and bayed and snarled while they rolled and scooped. Some people put on a great show and everyone laughed and laughed. They'd think of the most comical things to do."

Food—or the search for it—motivates the leading character in the oral libraries of our great-grandfathers: Weget, the trickster-transformer. There are literally thousands of Weget stories, and most of them concern food.

Weget wanders through the generations, a hungry giant whose appetite is seldom satisfied and whose conscience is never troubled by the tricks he plays in futile attempts to fill his stomach. These tricks form—or transform—the people of the air, the water, the earth, and rearrange the geography. They are the tricks of a bumbler, rather than of an astute manipulator—a huge, handsome, hungry bumbler.

Are there other races whose leading cultural figure's prime concern is food? Whose leading cultural figure is a failure? The legends we have read from the literature of other races centre around warriors, kings, gods and other heroic figures. What does this tell us about ourselves? Are we more practical, more realistic, better able to laugh at ourselves? Whatever the answer, food certainly plays a major part in the mystery.

Some think that the food in the Weget stories is a symbol for all human greed and that Weget's consistent failures are lessons for those who crave wealth, prestige and domination over others. Whether or not this is the case, the food-seeking exploits of our culture hero—perhaps we should say culture clown—are another aspect of "How Food Shaped the Way of the Gitksan."

Appendices

The Writing System

In this book we have spelled Gitksan words using a modified roman alphabet of forty-six letters, set out below. This system was adapted by Jay Powell of the University of British Columbia from an earlier system developed by Lonnie Hindle and Bruce Rigsby. The earlier Hindle-Rigsby system is also still in common use, and the alternative forms which it includes are given below in brackets.

a	short A	'm [ṁ]	hard M
aa	long A	n	soft N
b	B	'n [ṅ]	hard N
d	D	o	short O
e	short E	oo	long O
ee	long E	p	soft P
g	front G	p'	hard P
gw	G-W	s	S
g̲	back G	t	soft T
h	H	t'	hard T
hl	H-L	tl'	hard T-L
i	short I	ts	soft T-S
ii	long I	ts'	hard T-S
j	J	u	short U
k	soft front K	uu	long U
k'	hard front K	w	soft W
kw	soft K-W	'w [ẇ]	hard W
kw'	hard K-W	x	front X
k̲	soft back K	xw	X-W
k̲'	hard back K	x̲	back X
l	soft L	y	soft Y
'l [l̇]	hard L	'y [ẏ]	hard Y
m	soft M	'	glottal stop

Gitxsanimx̲, the language of the Gitksan, lacks several sounds which are common in English; thus the Gitksan alphabet contains no *f, v, r* or *z*. On the other hand, the language does contain a number of sounds not found in English, and to represent these sounds we use modified forms of the usual roman letters.

Like Navajo and several other American Indian languages, the Gitksan tongue distinguishes between "hard" and "soft" consonants. The hard consonants are the ones that linguists call glottalized consonants. They usually sound as though they are popped or exploded. It is easy to test whether you are glottalizing or "hardening" these consonants when you pronounce them. Simply place your finger on your Adam's apple while you speak. Your Adam's apple should jump up momentarily as you pronounce a hard consonant. These consonants are indicated in the writing system by the addition of an apostrophe: k', k̲', kw', p', t', tl', and 'l, 'm, 'n, 'w, 'y.

Where the apostrophe appears in conjunction with one of the consonants just listed, it always indicates a glottalized consonant. In other combinations (usually between two vowels) the apostrophe indicates a glottal stop. Consider for example the word *nisk'o'o,* meaning thimbleberry. Here the second apostrophe indicates a glottal stop. This sound is common in Arabic, Hebrew and many other languages. It also appears regularly in Scots pronunciation and other British dialects, and almost all English speakers use it on occasion for emphasis. Say "Out!" very forcefully, or say, for instance, "an *ice* house, not a *nice* house," and listen for the sudden release or catch at the beginning of word *out* or the word *ice*. That is the glottal stop.

The Gitksan language also distinguishes between certain front and back consonants. Our letter **g** is pronounced like the hard English *g* in the word *girl*. Our letter **g̲** is pronounced much the same but farther back in the throat. In the same way we distinguish between **k** and **k̲**, between **k'** and **k̲'**, and between **x** and **x̲**.

These last two letters, **x** and **x̲**, represent *h*-like sounds not found in English. The **x** is pronounced like the *ch* in German words such as *ich* or *Bach,* and **x̲** represents a similar sound pronounced farther back in the throat.

Like classical Greek, Gitxsanimx̲ distinguishes between short and long vowels. In writing, we indicate the long vowels simply by writing them twice.

Terminology

Here is a list of the Gitksan words used in this book, together with their approximate English translations. In the case of plant names, the botanical Latin designations are also given wherever possible. Alternate pronunciations are shown in parentheses.

Words on this list are alphabetized according to the Gitksan alphabet outlined in the previous section. Thus, words beginning with *aa* follow those beginning with *a*, and words beginning with *hl* follow those beginning with *h*.

A

adaawk (adaawkx) family history

aksa maa'y berry juice

am sk'iikx smoked fish eggs

anjam pot; cooking vessel

anyoo barbecue stake

anyuusim gan wooden food cache

anyuusim yip earth cellar

anyust cellar; hiding place

ax bulblet fern (*Cystopteris bulbifera*)

AA

aatk'yasxw the visible embodiment of a doctor's curing power.

B

bagwanswx welcome feast

batsa special gift; *literally,* to lift up something

bii 'yan whole undressed fish

buts' (daadooxw) L-shaped piece in stomach of fish

D

damtx fiddlehead fern

dayks dessert made with snow, water and berries

dilawsa (delawasa) gooseberry

do'o fish cheek

G

gim dii yee 'asxw pack relay system

gusiit (squsiit) potato

gyaba' ladleful of food; special gift for highest chiefs

gyam serviceberry or saskatoon berry (*Amelanchier alnifolia*)

G̲

ga geekx (ga geekx) waxy substance in nose of fish

gahlgoosxw tied bunches of fish (usually 40) ready for, or already in, the final drying stage in the smokehouse

gale'e (k'alamst) wild rose seeds

gal k'oop (gal k'an) baked fish hearts

gan geeluxw cooking rack

ganiis dog salmon

gan hix pine noodles

gan ts'al filleting board

gap pile of 40 fish

gasx wild rice (chocolate lily, *Fritillaria camchatcensis*) having unpleasant odour

gatl'okwots short wild rhubarb (young cow parsnip, *Heracleum lanatum*)

gax lakws heavily smoked fish

go goyp (gap goop) bunchberries (*Cornus canadensis*)

H

hagehlast   scraper

hagul jam   slow boil

ha la mootxw   oolichan grease; *literally, "for curing humanity"*

halayt   medicine man or woman

ha'nii bahla'am ts'al   hand-held toasting racks made from willow withes

ha'nii yats is   partially sewn cedar mat into which soapberry pickers "hit" the berries

hayxw   after-life "spirit"

huxws   fish strips or parings

HL

hlabal weex   enamel cup

hlayax   fruit coated with oolichan grease

I

is   soapberries (*Shepherdia canadensis*)

J

jamksxw   boiled, fully dried salmon

jam k'yo'o   boiled fish backbone

K'

k'ay yuxws   fish strips

k'itsa'i   roast marrow

K'

k'ots   false Solomon's seal

k'ots maa'y   cut berry cakes

L

logwolan   matured fish eggs

loots'   elderberries (*Sambucus racemosa*)

luu 'lanim hlok'asxw   boiled salmon eggs and seaweed

'L

'lana t'im ges   matured fish eggs and heads

M

maa'y tsa   small chunks of dried berries (saskatoons)

milkst   crab apples

maawin   juice of the horsetail reed (*Equisetum hyemale*)

mismuus   cow

moohl   fish trap

mo'onim hon   salted fish

mo'onim ts'okxw   salted fish belly

moosxan   toasted suet on a stick; a special treat in ancient times

'M

'mii gan   high bush blueberries (*Vaccinium ovalifolium*)

'mii ganaa'w   frogberries (dewberries) (*Rubus chamaemorus*)

'mii gunt   strawberry

'mii k'ooxst   salmonberries (*Rubus spactabilis*)

'mii oot   low bush cranberries (*Vaccinium vitis-idaea*)

'mii ooyak'   baked in hot coals

'mii yahl   low bush blueberries

N

naasikx   raspberry

Nax Nok (Lax Nokx)   Power-Beyond-the-Human

nisk'o'o   thimbleberry (*Rubus parviflorus*)

'N

'nii bahla'am ts'al   toasted half-dried fish

'niist   to smear with soapberry foam

P

pt'ikxw   cleaned fish (head and guts removed) ready to put in smokehouse for drying before filleting, or whole fish drying prior to filleting

P'

p'ah'loosxw   fried seaweed

S

sa'uyasxw oolichan grease-preparing process

sa xulgwa toasted seaweed

sim maa'y huckleberry (*Vaccinium parviflorum*)

si'moogit (sim'oogit) chief

sibim gal ts'ap village soup

sk'an dax do'oxwhl Labrador tea (*Ladum groenlandicum*)

sk'yanadoos swamp spruce gum

snaaw pinchberry (Western bitter cherry, *Prunus emarginata*)

snax thornberry (*Crataegus douglasii*)

so'o food to take home, or taken home, from a feast

statxs nettles

T

thets chief's messengers; invitation bearers

tkwa'ltxw plantain (*Plantago major*)

T'

t'axwinst adze

t'in fish weirs

t'ip yeest stonecrop (*Sedum divergens*)

t'imii'it kinnikinnick (bearberry, *Arctostaphylos uva-ursi*)

t'ul triangular piece at neck of a fish

t'uuts'xwa maa'y blackberry

TL'

tl'okxw shame feast

TS'

ts'a'a eyes (of fish or other animal)

ts'anks sa gaakx wild onion

ts'eewa gax fried rabbit intestines

ts'idipxst cranberries

ts'ilimdinhl to make a pack lunch for someone other than yourself to take on a journey

ts'im xts'axs spaces in smokehouse

ts'okxw centre of fish belly (portion containing two fins)

ts'ook (mii ts'ookxw) chokecherry (*Prunus virginiana*)

UU

uuda t'im ges baked fish heads

W

wilp ha'nii jokx hunting cabin (house-for-all-the-world)

wilp sa hon smokehouse

wilp sa maa'y berry drying houses

win do'o substance producing sleep

wit crossbars in smokehouse, used for drying rack

'W

'witsxw maa'y crushed berries

X

xsuu'w baked hemlock bark

X̱

x̱ay mooxws mixture of sugar, snow, soaked dried berries, oolichan grease; specialty of Wolves of Kuldo

x̱gal'inkx gift-payment of apples, oranges, distributed at feasts

x̱hlaxws small skewers for serving first salmon of year

x̱mihl consuming overheated fish

x̱sax t'iisa' pan bread, unkneaded

x̱so'omsxw consuming *so'o* (small village feast)

x̱s'winkx herring eggs

x̱'witsansxw (x̱'witsxw) to give out the crushed berries

Y

yal is whipped soapberries; soapberry or frothberry foam

yoos hon dressed, fresh fish, barbecued or being barbecued

yukxw feast

Acknowledgements

The Book Builders owe much to some who do not live in the land of the 'Ksan.

We could not have put this book together without advice, support and countless photographs from the National Museum of Man. The British Columbia Provincial Museum, too, met without hesitation our pleas for photographs.

Our gratitude goes also to three linguists—Lonnie Hindle, Bruce Rigsby and Jay Powell—for devising writing systems which have enabled us to put words from our language onto paper. Most of the terminology used in this book was kindly checked by Dr. Powell.

Hilary Stewart's improvements to our drawings and her sensitive fulfillment of our verbal descriptions add a great deal. Thank you, Hilary.

THE BOOK BUILDERS OF 'KSAN

Charlotte Angus
James Angus
Norma Barnes
Richard Benson
Mary Blackwater
Martha Brown (Hazelton)
Martha Brown (Glen Vowell)
Tony Brown
Abel Campbell
Edith Campbell
Joshua Campbell
Sadie Daniels
Freda Diesing
Neil Erickson
James Fowler
Fred Good
Marie-Françoise Guédon
David Gunanoot
Chris Harris
Clara Harris
Sadie Harris
Ernest Hyzims
Lorraine Jack
Solomon Jack
Alice Jeffrey
Doreen Jensen
Charles Johnson
Ellen Johnson
Evelyn Johnson
Fred Johnson
Gideon Johnson
Lloyd Johnson

Maggie Johnson
Mary Johnson
Louise Joseph
Dorothy Lattie
Evie Lattie
Emily Latz
Sarah Marshall
Danny Matthews
Connie Milton
David Milton
George Milton
Johnny Moore
Geoffrey Morgan
Jack Morgan
Peggy Morgan
Reggie Morgan
Wallace Morgan
Willis Morgan
Elsie Morrison
Gertie Morrison
Moses Morrison
Steven Morrison
Arthur Mowatt
Jane Mowatt
Mary Mowatt
Sophia Mowatt
Ester Muldoe
Lottie Muldoe
Shirley Muldon
Edith McDougal
Mary McKenzie
Norman McLean

James McRae
Irene Ness
Irene Patsy
Marilyn Robinson
Olive Ryan
Jackie Rusell
Arthur Sampson
Mary Sampson
Perry Sampson
Polly Sargent
Barbara Sennott
Fanny Smith
Joe Smith
Art Sterritt
Barbara E. Sterritt
Jessie Sterritt
Patsy Sterritt
Charles Stevens
Russell Stevens
Agnes Sutton
Agnes Travers
Cliff Weeks
Alice Williams
Johnson Williams
Doris Wilson
Gordon Wilson
Laurel Wilson
Marie Wilson
Walter Wilson, Jr.
Walter Wilson, Sr.
James Woods
Henry Wright